In easy steps is an imprint of Computer Step
Southfield Road . Southam
Warwickshire CV47 0FB . United Kingdom
www.ineasysteps.com

Notice of Liability

Every effort has been made to ensure that this book contains accurate and current information. However, Computer Step and the author shall not be liable for any loss or damage suffered by readers as a result of any information contained herein.

Trademarks

Microsoft® and Windows® are registered trademarks of Microsoft Corporation. All other trademarks are acknowledged as belonging to their respective companies.

Printed and bound in the United Kingdom

ISBN 1-84078-150-5

Contents

3 C# Language Essentials 51

4 Object Essentials 75

Getting Started

This chapter gives an overview of C#, including Visual C# installation, getting to know the development environment, and getting started writing your first applications.

Covers

Chapter One

Introduction

C# is the best way to write programs for Windows and the Internet. But why write a program? Simply, because it gives you the maximum control over your computer. Programs can automate your work, preventing mistakes and making you more productive. Programming is fun as well!

C# is a young language, and benefits from current thinking about how to help programmers write applications that are reliable and effective. It is also fully up-to-date with the Internet era, so it is equally suitable whether your programs run for one person on a desktop, or communicate with other computers on a network or even around the world.

This book covers Microsoft Visual C# .NET, the main C# implementation, available in several versions:

- Visual C# Standard Edition is ideal for beginners. Everything you need to create Windows programs is included

- Visual Studio .NET includes an enhanced version of Visual C# as well as other languages like C++, Visual Basic, and the Java-like J#. The Professional Edition is a complete development bundle

- Visual Studio .NET Enterprise Developer adds features like source code control, and comes with development versions of Windows server products. The Enterprise Architect version adds modelling tools and other high-end features

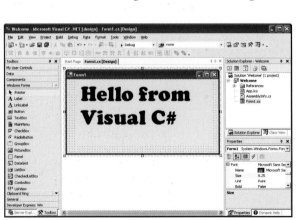

Visual C# is both easy and powerful

C# and other languages

The term "Visual C#" means the C# language combined with the Visual Studio development tools. The language itself is simply called C#.

The first full release of C# was in late 2001. It is a relatively new language, but designed to be familiar to programmers who know C or C++. The Java language is also based on C, so it is easy for Java developers to learn C#. As a language, C# is elegant, simple, powerful, and fully object-oriented. Its clean design makes it a good choice for new programmers.

C and C++ are excellent languages in the hands of skilled programmers, but also have a reputation for being difficult to learn. By contrast, C# is C++ made easy. Memory management is automatic, pointers are rarely used, and there are no header files or #define macros. Visual C# also benefits from the visual development tools in Visual Studio, which let you assemble forms and web pages by drag-and-drop. Visual C# combines the productivity of Visual Basic with a C-style language.

To run Visual C# you need Windows NT 4.0, 2000 or XP. It does not run on Windows 95, 98 or ME. However, applications compiled with Visual C# do run on Windows 98 and ME (but not Windows 95).

Visual C# compiles applications for Microsoft's .NET Framework. This gives you access to a rich set of components and functions, as well as providing security and reliability features. Microsoft calls this "Managed code", meaning that the .NET runtime manages the security, memory usage, and performance optimization of your programs. In order to run a Visual C# application, the .NET Framework must be installed. This is free to distribute, and Microsoft includes it automatically with the latest versions of Windows, but it is an important consideration if you want to install your applications on a wide range of systems.

Here are some of the reasons why it is worth programming in Visual C#:

- Programming powerful Web applications is almost as easy as programming for Windows

- Visual C# is fully object-oriented. What this means is explained in chapter 4. It also makes Visual C# a good language for learning how to program

- Visual C# is extensively used by Microsoft itself, making it the premier language for the .NET Framework and Windows now and in the future

Installing Visual C#

Installing Visual C# (or the complete Visual Studio) is a matter of running setup from the first CD in your installation pack and following the directions, which will vary according to what is already installed on your machine.

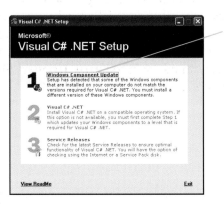

You may need to install the Component Update. This is a set of system files used both by Visual C# and other Windows software.

If you are not sure about whether to install a Web server, continue without it. Visual C# will still work, and you can install a Web server later if you want. If you are on a network, there may be an Internet Information Services Web server on another machine you can use instead. The reason for caution is that running a Web server can be a security risk when you connect to the Internet.

2 With Visual C# you can build dynamic Web applications. These require a Web server, so you have the option to install one on your own machine. If you do this, pay careful attention to the security notes. Otherwise, just click Continue: Visual C# will still work, and you can install the Web server later if you want.

3 Select which components you need. The documentation takes a lot of space. Uncheck some of the options if you need to.

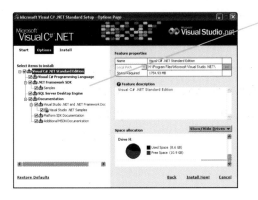

Making sense of the IDE

To run Visual C#, run Microsoft Visual Studio .NET from the Programs group of the Start menu.

When you run Visual C#, it opens up in an application called an IDE, which stands for "Integrated Development Environment." This consists of a central work area surrounded by tool windows and with a menu and toolbars at the top. The docked tool windows can be "torn off" as floating windows, or hidden altogether. You can also have them partially hidden, so they pop out when the mouse hovers over their button at the border of the IDE. This is called an Auto Hide window. The central work area is tabbed, and the tabs can take you to visual designers like the form editor, and text editors.

There are many different ways to lay out the Visual Studio IDE, and different versions of Visual C# and Visual Studio have different features. That means the illustrations in this book may not look exactly the same as what appears on your screen. However, the steps given here will apply whatever layout you use.

Menu bar	Toolbars	Tabbed work area	Docked tool window	Auto-hidden window

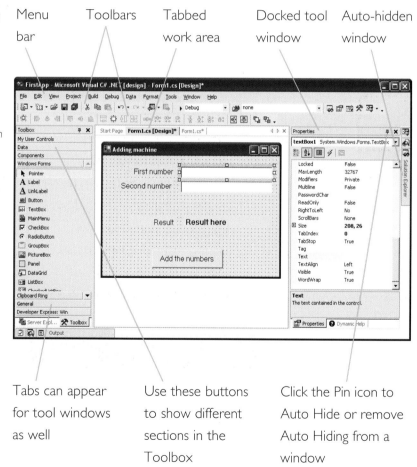

There is an option to run the IDE in "Tabbed Document" or "MDI" mode. Tabbed Document is preferred and is the default, but you might want to experiment. You can also reset the window layout to the default, if it gets untidy. These options are in Tools > Options > Environment > General.

Tabs can appear for tool windows as well

Use these buttons to show different sections in the Toolbox

Click the Pin icon to Auto Hide or remove Auto Hiding from a window

Your first application

To get started with Visual C#, here is how to create an application in four easy steps:

 By using events, properties and methods you can bring your forms to life. This chapter begins to show you how to do this, using step-by-step examples.

1 Start Visual C# or Visual Studio and click the New Project icon, or choose New - Project from the File menu.

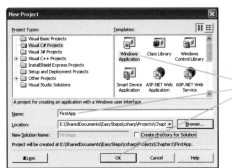

2 In the New Project dialog click on Windows Application. Then type FirstApp in the Name box. Next, click OK to start the project.

 If you cannot find the Properties window, or any of the other main Visual C# windows, choose it from the View menu. Then it will pop back into view. You can also press F4 to show the Properties window.

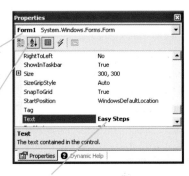

3 A window opens, called Form1. In the Properties window, make sure that Form1 shows in the top drop-down. Sort the properties alphabetically, by clicking the AZ button. Then find the entry for Text, and type over Form1 so it says Easy Steps.

 In this book, the illustrations show the Properties window sorted alphabetically. If you prefer, you can sort by categories, but the list will then be in a different order from the illustrations.

4 In the Toolbar, click the Start button (small right arrow) to run. This first application just creates a window. It is a proper one. You can resize, move or minimize it, and finally quit the application by closing it. It may not do much but you've just created a Windows program!

First look at the Toolbox

Visual C#'s Toolbox contains the building bricks of your applications. In the following example, you use the toolbox to add some text to the form created on the previous page.

While you work in Visual C#, the Pointer icon will be selected most of the time. Only select the other icons in the Toolbox when you want to place a new object on a form.

Click the "A" icon on the Toolbox. This is the icon for a label. It will change appearance to show it is selected.

The exact contents of the Toolbox vary according to which version of Visual C# you have and how you have set it up. If you right-click the Toolbox, you will see a menu that lets you add and remove the Toolbox components.

Move the mouse pointer over the form, and press down the left mouse button where you want to position the top-left corner of the label. Keep it pressed down as you drag the mouse down and right to enlarge the label. Then release the button. If it is not quite right, you can move it with the mouse, or resize it using one of the eight resize tabs.

Resize tabs

First look at the Property Editor

Visual Studio's Property Editor is a list of characteristics. Each characteristic or "property" affects the currently selected object, such as a label or button, on a form. By changing these properties, you control the appearance of the object.

Changing the properties of a label

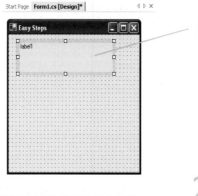

Drag a label from the Toolbox onto a form. You can use the example from the previous page if you like. Make sure the label is selected.

Now click in the right-hand column of the Properties window to change some values:

- Change BorderStyle to "FixedSingle"
- Expand Font, change size to 24
- Change Text to "My custom label"
- Change TextAlign to "TopCenter" (click on the center block in the drop-down image)

Notice how the appearance of the label alters to reflect your changes

Getting to know Visual C# forms

Web applications aside, most Visual C# applications are based on a form. The form is a canvas on which you paint your application. In many cases, there will be more than one form, and Visual C# lets you display and hide forms while the application is running. Closing the main form quits the application.

A form is a window. That is why forms have Minimize, Maximize and Close buttons, just like other kinds of window.

Like all Visual C# objects, forms have properties. To select a form, so that its properties appear in the Properties window, click anywhere on the background of a form.

Key form properties

Icon: small picture that appears at top-left or when the form is minimized

Text: words that appears in the title bar of the form

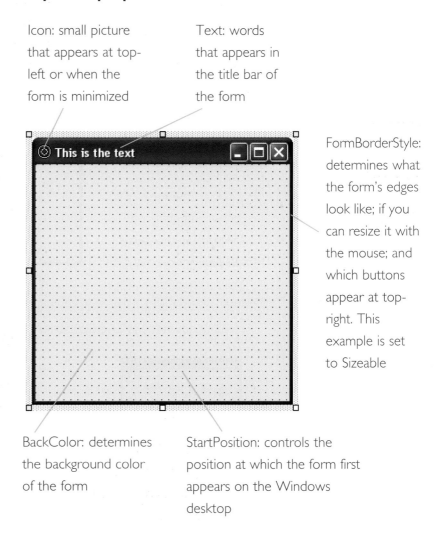

This is the text

FormBorderStyle: determines what the form's edges look like; if you can resize it with the mouse; and which buttons appear at top-right. This example is set to Sizeable

BackColor: determines the background color of the form

StartPosition: controls the position at which the form first appears on the Windows desktop

Placing a button

A button is one of the most useful objects. Buttons put the user in control of your application. Using Visual C#, you determine what happens when the user clicks the button with the mouse.

Placing a button on a form

To make the illustration easier to read, I have increased the font size for the label and the form. To do this, edit the Font property in the Properties window. If you click the + symbol to the left of the Font property, this shows sub-properties including the Size, which you can then change.

When you change the Font properties of the form itself, all controls on the form take on the form's new font, unless you specifically set a different one. Properties that behave like this are called "ambient."

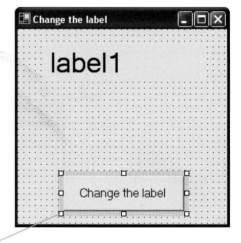

Click the Button icon in the Toolbox so that it is depressed.

2 Click on the form, drag down and right, and release the mouse to place a button. You can resize the button with the resize tabs or move it by clicking on the middle of the button, holding down the left mouse button and then dragging.

When you type text for a button, menu or other control, the & character has a special meaning. The & does not display. Instead, the following character is underlined. By pressing the Alt key in combination with the underlined character, the object can be clicked without using the mouse. This is called a keyboard shortcut.

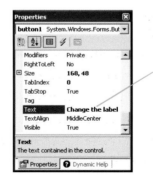

3 Use the Properties window to make the button's Text read "Change the label".

First look at events

Most Windows software works by responding to the actions of the user. For example, when you press a key in a word processor, a character appears in a document. An event (pressing a key) is followed by a response (the document is updated).

This process of responding to events is vital for creating Visual C# applications. You write instructions to be carried out when a particular event occurs. A classic example is clicking a button.

You do not have to double-click to open the code editor. Instead, you can right-click an object and choose View Code from the pop-up menu that appears. If you use this technique, Visual C# does not generate any additional code.

You can get back to the visual form designer by clicking the tab that has the same name as the code file, but followed by the word "[Design]".

Once the code editor is open, you can use the tabs to switch between design and code view.

To see how this works, place a button on a form, or use the example from the previous page. Now double-click the button with the mouse. Visual C# opens a text editor, with some text already entered. It looks like this:

```
private void button1_Click(object sender,
    System.EventArgs e)

    {

    }
```

You will write code between the curly brackets that will run when the button gets clicked.

Double-click a button to open the code editor, ready for you to type in your code. To get started, this is where you type, between the curly brackets.

A function that responds to an event is called an Event handler. In programming, "handling" an event means writing code that runs when the event occurs.

Buttons can respond to other events as well. To see all the events, select the button in the Properties window and click the Events icon (it looks like a lightning flash). If you double-click in the right hand space next to an event, it creates skeleton code to respond to that event.

Your first line of code

To try this example, you need a form with a button and a label. You can continue the example from the previous page.

1 Open the code editor for the Click event by double-clicking the button in the designer.

2 Type "label1." (not forgetting the dot). A drop-down menu appears. Type "t" and the list jumps to the T section. Use the down arrow to move to Text so it is highlighted. Press the Spacebar, and the word "Text" is automatically entered.

The coding feature used here is called Auto List Members. Although it is handy, some people find it annoying. If so, you can switch it off using the Options dialog, available from the Tools menu. In the Options dialog, you need to find the Tab for Text Editor > C# > Auto List Members.

```
private void button1_Click(object sender, System.EventArgs e)
{
    label1.t
}
```

SizeChanged
StyleChanged
SuspendLayout
SystemColorsChanged
TabIndex
TabIndexChanged
Tag
Text   string Control.Text
TextAlign   Gets or sets the text associated with this control.
TextAlignChanged

3 Complete the line of code by typing so it reads:

```
label1.Text = "I've been changed";
```

It is important to include the final semicolon.

You can also select a property in an Auto List Members list by double-clicking on the property you want.

Change the label

I've been changed

Change the label

4 Run the application by clicking the Start button on Visual Studio's toolbar. Now click the button. The label's caption changes.

Setting properties in code

Let's look a little closer at the code you wrote for the button's Click event. Here it is again:

```
label1.Text = "I've been changed";
```

Now, you could have created a label with this caption another way. If you selected the label, and typed into the Text property in the Properties window, that would have the same result.

The example on this page shows how you can set properties for alignment and color. These properties are really numbers, but to make them easier to remember you can use constants like Color.Yellow instead. Auto List Members shows what constants are available.

The code you wrote tells C# to set the Text property of the object called label1 to the value "I've been changed".

The advantage of setting property values in code is that you don't need to know beforehand what the values will be. You can determine them at runtime. You can see this working in the next application.

In the meantime, try setting some more label properties in code to see how effective this can be:

C# is case-sensitive. That means you must always use the same combination of capital letters and lower case letters when referring to an object name, or any variable or C# keyword. For example, if you type Label1, the code will not run and Visual C# will report a Build error.

Type in and run this example to show how you can set the properties of a Visual C# object in code. Use Auto List Members to save typing long expressions like ContentAlignment.TopRight;

```
Start Page │ End Statement │ Form1.cs [Design]* │ Form1.cs*          ◁ ▷ ✕

ChangeLabel.Form1                    ▼   Main()                      ▼

    private void button1_Click(object sender, System.EventArg
    {
        label1.Text = "I've been changed";
        label1.TextAlign = ContentAlignment.TopRight;
        label1.BackColor = Color.Yellow;
        label1.ForeColor = Color.Blue;
        label1.Font = new Font("Arial",12,FontStyle.Italic);
    }
```

A C# adding machine

This example is more interesting, in that it performs a useful function. It adds two numbers and displays the result. It introduces a new object, the TextBox.

Creating the adding machine

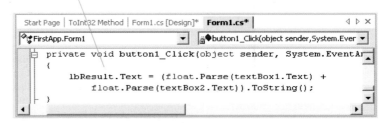

1 This is a TextBox in the Toolbox window. Add two of them to a form and set the Text property to nothing.

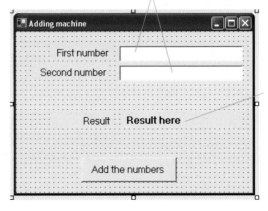

2 Next add 4 labels and a button as shown.

3 Set this label's name property to lbResult using the Properties window (see page 14 for an example).

4 There is just one line of code for the button's Click event:

```
lbResult.Text = (float.Parse(textBox1.Text) +
float.Parse(textBox2.Text)).ToString();
```

Don't worry if the code looks puzzling – it's explained in Chapter 3.

Start Page | ToInt32 Method | Form1.cs [Design]* | **Form1.cs***

FirstApp.Form1 ▼ | button1_Click(object sender, System.Ever ▼

```
private void button1_Click(object sender, System.EventAr
{
    lbResult.Text = (float.Parse(textBox1.Text) +
        float.Parse(textBox2.Text)).ToString();
}
```

5 Now test the application by clicking the Start button. Type a number in each of the TextBoxes, and click the button to add the two together and show the result.

Dealing with errors

We all make mistakes. What happens if you try to run an application that contains typing errors or faulty code? For example, what if you typed `textBox1.Txt` instead of `textBox1.Text`? In most cases, Visual C# will halt and display an error message. Then it will show the line of code which caused the error.

1 Visual C# stops and displays an error message:

If you click on an error in the Task List, and then press F1, Visual C# will often display a detailed Help entry that explains more about the error and how to fix it.

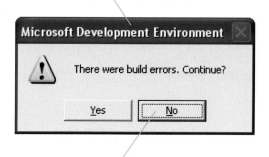

2 Click No. Then look at the Task List which pops up with a list of errors.

3 Double-click an error in the Task List to jump to that point in the code.

You can write code to catch errors and make your programs more robust. This is introduced in Chapter 6.

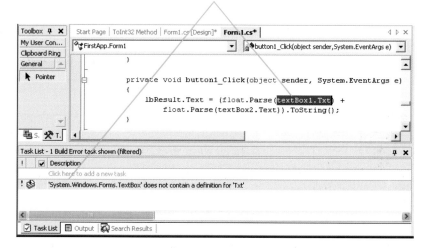

How to get Help

There's a lot to remember in Visual C# and some operations are complex. It is important to learn how to use the online Help. Because Visual C# is very popular, there are lots of other sources of assistance, including books, magazines and discussions on the Internet.

Help through ToolTips

Let the mouse hover over an icon to show a ToolTip

The online help documents are mainly from MSDN ("Microsoft Developer Network"). From the Help menu, choose Contents to open the online version of Visual C#'s manuals and other manuals and articles. Online help is integrated with MSDN, so that when you press F1 you actually find an MSDN article.

Help through Visual C# Help

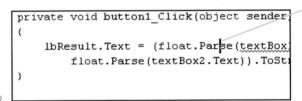

Place the cursor in the word for which you want help.

MSDN contains a huge amount of information. Set "Filtered by" to Visual C# to find the key Visual C# entries quickly. If it is slow, run Setup again and choose to copy more of MSDN to your hard disk for better performance, provided of course you have plenty of free disk space.

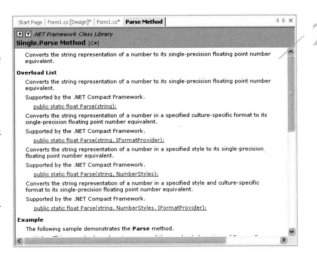

Press F1 to bring up help on that particular word, if available.

Searching Help

This is a short book but even a long one can't contain all the detail in online Help. The problem is finding the right entry. It is hard because the MSDN library (online Help) supplied with Visual C# covers many languages and topics (including C++ and other languages). Here are some tips on finding the right information:

How to search Help

When you search online Help, try to narrow down the search by including several words. You can use quotation marks to search for an expression of more than one word, such as "Visual C#", as well as the AND, OR, NOT operators. You can also set a filter. Here is an example:

Along with search, there is also a Help index (Help > Index). Use this with filters for the best results. If you want help on a Visual C# keyword, placing the cursor on the word in the editor and pressing F1 is often the quickest way to find it.

Imagine you want help on the Image property of a PictureBox. From the Help menu, choose Search or press Ctrl+Alt+F3. Type words into the search box. If you just type "Image Property", the maximum 500 topics are returned, most of little relevance

When you search for several words, the AND operator is implied by default. Use OR if you want the maximum number of results.

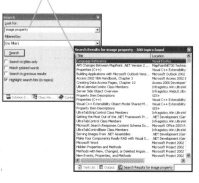

If you type "Image Property PictureBox C#" you find just 102 topics, many of which are relevant

Setting a filter is a lengthy operation. However, once set, it performs well until you change it. The exact numbers of results on your system may vary, as MSDN is updated regularly.

If you add a filter for "Visual C#", it narrows to just 51 topics.

Double-click an entry to show the document.

First look at the Solution Explorer

A Visual C# application can contain more than one form. It can also include modules of pure code, not attached to any form, and several other more advanced elements. Managing the items in a large project can get difficult. The Solution Explorer is a window which lists all the items in your project. If the Solution Explorer is not visible, select it from the View menu or press Ctrl+Alt+l.

If you can't see the Solution Explorer, Properties Window, Toolbox, or other Visual C# windows, then you can use the View menu to bring them back.

Click here to view the code editor for the selected object

Click here to view the object itself, for example a form

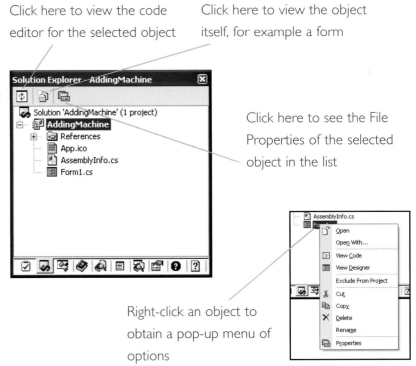

Click here to see the File Properties of the selected object in the list

Right-click an object to obtain a pop-up menu of options

When to use the Solution Explorer

Use the Solution Explorer when you want to view an object such as a form or code module. These are not always visible, even when a project is loaded. By using the Solution Explorer you can keep an uncluttered screen, just viewing the particular objects you are working on.

If you have a large project, the Solution Explorer is essential for finding the form or code which you need to work on next. You can also open several related projects at once, which is why it is called the Solution Explorer instead of the Project Explorer.

Saving your project

Visual C# always creates a new folder (directory) for a Visual C# project. This makes it easy to manage your work – for example, moving, deleting or backing-up the project.

A Visual C# project consists of more than one file when saved to disk. For example, the simplest Windows Form project contains a project file, with the extension .csproj, a form file, with the extension .cs, and a number of other files.

When you chose Save from the File menu only the file currently active is saved. To save an entire project, choose Save All. If you close Visual C# you will be prompted to save any unsaved files.

By default, files are saved automatically when you run a project. This helps to avoid losing work if something goes wrong, but can work against you if you deleted code by accident.

The name of a file is determined by the name you choose when adding a new item, such as a form or module. To change the file name, select it in the Solution Explorer and choose Properties. Note that the File Properties are different from the regular Properties for an object.

If you want to change the name of a file in a project, it is best to do this from the Solution Explorer rather than searching for the file on disk and renaming it directly. Otherwise, Visual C# will think the file is missing next time you open the project.

On the other hand, If you want to make a copy of an entire project, simply copy the directory from outside Visual C#, and open the copy you have made.

How to change the file name of a form

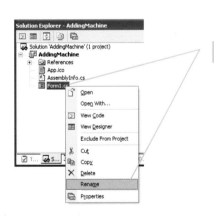

Open the Solution Explorer, right-click the form in the list, and choose Rename.

2 Click here to type in a new name for the form. You should use the extension .cs. Visual C# will rename the actual file behind the scenes.

Reopening an application

To reopen a Visual C# project, use the following steps:

Visual C# also lets you open projects and solutions through File > Recent Projects, and through the Start Page which lists the projects you have been working on.

1 Choose Open > Project from the File menu.

2 Find the project file (with a .csproj extension) or the solution file (with a .sln extension) and click on it to highlight it.

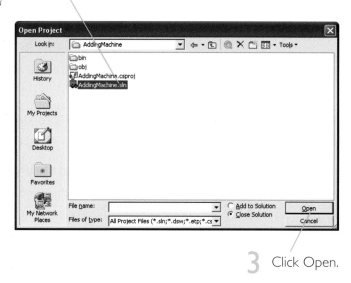

3 Click Open.

Opening more than one project at once

Visual C# lets you open more than one project at once. To do this, select Add to Solution when you open a project. It will be added to the projects already open in Visual C#.

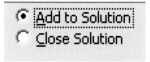

Project or solution?

A solution is a container for one or more projects. If you open a solution, all the projects it contains will be opened. When the solution contains a single project, it often makes little difference whether you open the solution or the project it contains. However, solutions can contain files and settings that are outside any project, so it is normally preferable to work with the solution.

Controls Explained

Through the .NET Framework, Visual C# gives you a wide range of pre-defined objects which you can use to assemble an application. This chapter describes each of the key objects in the Visual C# Toolbox.

Covers

Chapter Two

Controls and methods

The objects in the Visual C# Toolbox are often called controls. Most of the controls represent things that will be familiar to you if you have worked with other Windows applications.

We saw in Chapter One that controls have properties which determine their appearance and how they work. Controls also have events, actions that trigger a response. Before looking more closely at individual examples, there is another feature of Visual C# controls with which you need to be familiar – the concept of methods.

What is a method?

If you look up a control in Visual C# Help, you will see that Properties, Events and Methods are listed. Together, these tell you almost everything about what the control can do. The easiest way to find the help entry is to click on the button with the mouse so it is selected, and then press F1.

A property is something an object *has*. By contrast, a method is something that it *does*.

For example, a motor vehicle has properties, like color, model, age and speed. But what about starting and stopping? These are things that a vehicle does. If a vehicle were a Visual C# object, Start and Stop would be two of its methods. Often, methods have extra information called parameters. These appear in brackets after the method name, and specify how the action is to take place. For example, a vehicle might stop quickly or slowly. Even when there are no parameters, you still need to include the brackets.

An example

Labels have a Hide method which makes them invisible, and a Show method that makes them visible.

You could put a second button on the form that runs label1.Show(), in order to show the label again. Hiding and showing objects is a handy technique to learn.

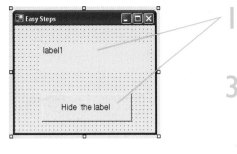

1 Place a label and a button on a form.

3 Run the application and click the button.

2 In the button's Click event, type:

```
label1.Hide();
```

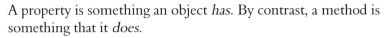

Using buttons

If you have worked through Chapter One, you will already be familiar with buttons. Use buttons when you want an easy way for users to kick off an operation, confirm or cancel a choice, or get help.

Most of your work with buttons involves setting properties and writing code for one event, Click.

The Text property determines what text appears on the button. Use the & character to create a keyboard shortcut

Use the sizing tabs to resize the button

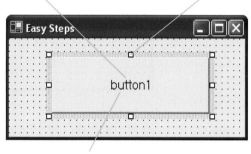

The Font property lets you change the font used for the caption

For a more interesting appearance, set the Image property to an image. Then set the ImageAlign property to TopCenter and TextAlign to BottomCenter. Make the button high enough to show both elements. You can even specify a list of images so that you can change them in code when the button is down or disabled.

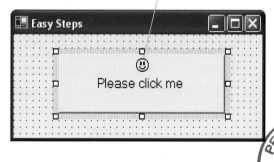

Using labels

Use labels to display text that the user does not need to edit. You can still change the text displayed from your code, by setting the Text property.

You can include an image in a label by setting the Image and ImageAlign properties

A white or colored background creates a more striking appearance

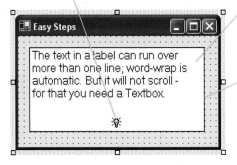

Set the BorderStyle property to FixedSingle for this boxed effect

How to align labels

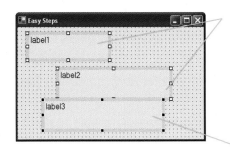

1 Place several labels on a form. Select all the ones you need to align by holding Shift down as you click on each in turn. The last one you select will be the master, to which the others align. Note the darker sizing tabs on this label.

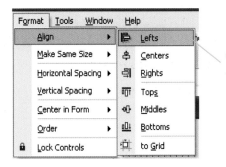

2 Choose Align from the Format menu. Choose Lefts from the submenu to align the labels to the left edge of the master.

Using TextBoxes

TextBoxes are an essential part of most Windows applications. The key difference between a label and a TextBox is that you can type into a TextBox at runtime. Another difference is that TextBoxes can display large amounts of text which the user can scroll through. TextBoxes were used in the Adding Machine application described in Chapter One.

Creating a scrollable TextBox

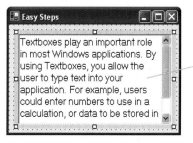

To create a scrollable TextBox, set its Multiline property to True and its ScrollBars property to Vertical

A letter-counting application

This example shows how to access a TextBox in code.

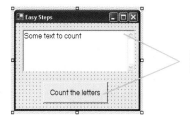

When you are typing code that refers to a control on a form, you can prevent errors by typing the word "this" followed by a dot. Auto-list members will pop up a list which includes the names of all the controls.

Auto-list members works with all the visible members of the class. See Chapter Four for an explanation of classes.

Place a TextBox and a button on a form.

Add this code to the button's Click event handler:

```
MessageBox.Show("You typed: " +
textBox1.Text.Length.ToString() + " characters.");
```

Test the application by running it, entering some text in the TextBox, and clicking the button.

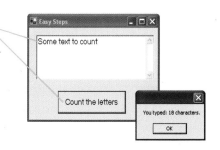

Using PictureBoxes

A PictureBox, as its name suggests, is a box which can contain a picture. Less obviously, you can draw on a PictureBox in your code.

Loading a picture

Not all picture files can be loaded directly into a PictureBox. In addition, there are many variations on even standard formats like .bmp or .wmf. If necessary, you can use additional software to convert pictures from one format to another.

Click the PictureBox icon in the Toolbox and place one on a form. Make sure it is selected.

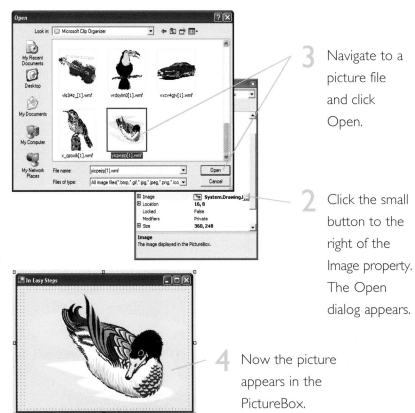

3 Navigate to a picture file and click Open.

2 Click the small button to the right of the Image property. The Open dialog appears.

If you cannot see the whole picture in the picture box, set the SizeMode to StretchImage. Then it is scaled to fit the box.

4 Now the picture appears in the PictureBox.

Which pictures can I load?

You can load bitmaps, icons and metafiles. Bitmaps must have a BMP, JPG, JPEG, GIF or PNG extension. Icons have an ICO extension. Metafiles have either a WMF or EMF extension. The advantage of metafiles is that you can scale the picture larger or smaller without loss of quality.

Using CheckBoxes

A CheckBox is a small box with a caption. When the user clicks the box, a check mark appears. Another click removes the mark.

If you have a set of options where the user may only choose one, use a RadioButton instead of a CheckBox.

CheckBoxes are ideal when you want to present a set of options from which the user can choose none, one, or more than one. In the example which follows, a pizza restaurant has a form for specifying which extra toppings the customer would like.

The Pizza application

1 Click the CheckBox icon in the Toolbox and place three on a form.

2 Add a label and button, setting the Text properties to some tempting pizza toppings. Name the CheckBoxes, for example chkMushrooms, chkHam and chkHot.

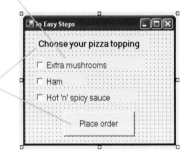

It doesn't matter if you can't yet follow the code in an application like this. C# code is tackled in the next chapter. For now, you only need to know what a CheckBox is for.

3 You can write code to find whether a box is checked by inspecting its Checked property. If it is True, then it is checked. This code is just the start, and only looks at the first CheckBox.

4 Enjoy your pizza!

Using RadioButtons

A RadioButton is like a CheckBox, but with one important difference: you can only have one button in a group checked. Checking a RadioButton automatically unchecks any others. For example, a pizza can be thin-crust or deep-pan, but not both.

Thin-crust or deep-pan?

When you lay out a group of option buttons, set the Checked property of one of them to True. Otherwise, when the application runs they will all be unchecked.

1 Click the RadioButton icon in the Toolbox and place two on a form.

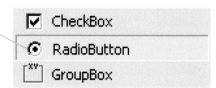

2 Add a label and a button and set the Text properties as shown. Name the buttons rbThin and rbDeep. Choose one of the RadioButtons and set the Checked property to True.

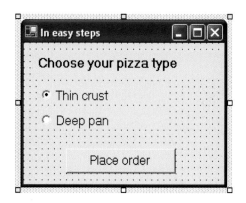

It is possible for all the RadioButtons to be unchecked, but only if they are all unchecked in the designer, or if you set all the Checked properties to false in your code. Once one is checked, the user cannot uncheck all of them using the mouse. This means you can use RadioButtons to force the user to choose one of the options.

3 Write code to inspect the Checked property of the RadioButtons. If it is True, then it is checked.

```csharp
private void button1_Click(object sender, System.EventArgs e)
{
    string sMessage;
    if (this.rbDeep.Checked)
    {
        sMessage = "You chose Deep Pan";
    }
    else if (this.rbThin.Checked)
    {
        sMessage = "You chose Thin Crust";
    }
    else
    {
        sMessage = "C'mon, make up your mind!";
    }

    MessageBox.Show(sMessage);
}
```

Using GroupBoxes

A GroupBox is a container for other objects. It is particularly useful for grouping objects that work together, like RadioButtons.

Pizzas in the box

You can check whether a control is in a GroupBox by moving the GroupBox. Controls that are in the GroupBox will move with it.

1 Click the GroupBox icon in the Toolbox and place two on a form.

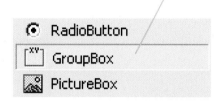

If you want two objects to match, like the GroupBoxes in this example, select them both together using Shift-click, and then use the Align and Make Same Size options.

2 Set the Text property for each GroupBox to describe its options.

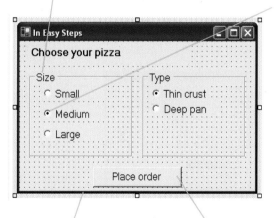

3 Click the RadioButton icon in the Toolbox and place buttons on each GroupBox. When placing the buttons, be sure your first click is on the GroupBox. Otherwise, the RadioButton will be on the form and not the GroupBox.

4 Try running the application and notice how the two groups of RadioButtons work independently.

5 You can write code for the Click event of this button to detect the choices made, by looking at the Checked property of each RadioButton.

Using ListBoxes

The ListBox is one of the most useful and powerful Visual C# controls. When you want to present choices to the user, a list is more flexible than a row of CheckBoxes or RadioButtons, because the number of items in the list can vary from one or two to many thousands. Databases like address books or business records often use lists to present the information.

Adding items to a ListBox

This is the first use in this book of a form's Load event. The Load event is ideal for placing code that runs before the user sees the form.

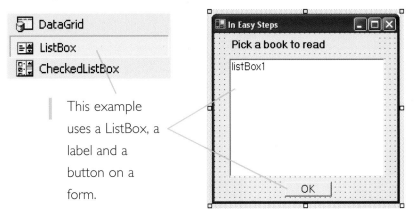

This example uses a ListBox, a label and a button on a form.

You can also fill a ListBox from the Properties window. The ListBox has an Items collection, and if you click this you can type entries directly into the list. It is usually more useful to fill the ListBox from code.

2 Set the ListBox's Sorted property to True, so that items in the list will be sorted alphabetically.

3 Double-click the form to open its Load event. Use the listBox.Items.Add method to add items to the ListBox. For example:

```
listBox1.Items.Add("C# in
Easy Steps");
```

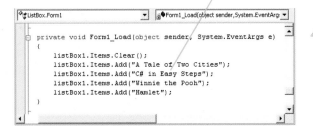

4 Run the application to see the ListBox filled.

ListBoxes are not restricted to storing strings. You can store almost any kind of object in a ListBox. The displayed value is that returned by the object's ToString() method.

It is no use adding items to a list unless you can tell which one the user has picked. There are two ways to do so. At runtime, the ListIndex property tells you which row in the list is selected, usually by the user clicking on that row. The Text property tells you the text in the selected row. If no row is selected, the ListIndex property is -1.

Retrieving an item from a ListBox

1 Your code should first check the SelectedIndex property. If it is -1, nothing is selected. If it is anything other than -1, use the Text property to find the contents of the chosen row.

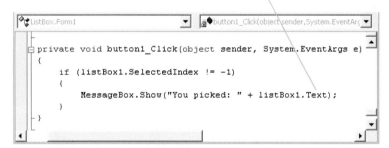

```
private void button1_Click(object sender, System.EventArgs e)
{
    if (listBox1.SelectedIndex != -1)
    {
        MessageBox.Show("You picked: " + listBox1.Text);
    }
}
```

If you wanted an item in the ListBox to be already selected when the form opens, you could set the SelectedIndex property in the Form Load event, like this:

```
listBox1.SelectedIndex
= 0;
```

(Note that the first item in the list is 0, not 1.)

2 Now run the application. If nothing is selected in the ListBox and you click OK, nothing happens. If a book title is selected, it appears in a message box when you click OK.

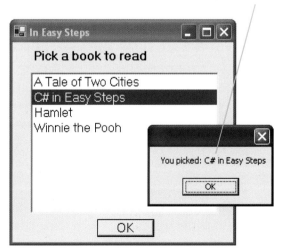

Using CheckedListBoxes

A CheckedListBox is an enhanced ListBox that lets you check and uncheck items in the list.

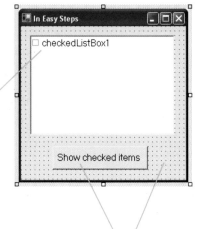

1 Place a CheckedListBox control and a button on a form. Set the CheckListBox's CheckOnClick property to True.

Without CheckOnClick set to True, the application will still work but the user will have to click twice to check an item, once to select it and a second time to check or uncheck.

2 Double-click the form to open its Load event handler, and the button to open its Click event handler. Then type this code, to load the items and then display the checked ones.

This code only works because the items stored in the ListBox are of type string. If the objects are of a different type, you would need to use the corresponding type for the item variable. See page 55 for more information about data types.

```
CheckedListBox.Form1                          Form1_Load(object sender, System.EventArgs e)

    private void Form1_Load(object sender, System.EventArgs e)
    {
        this.checkedListBox1.Items.Add("C# in Easy Steps");
        this.checkedListBox1.Items.Add("Windows XP in Easy Steps");
    }

    private void button1_Click(object sender, System.EventArgs e)
    {
        foreach (string item in this.checkedListBox1.CheckedItems )
        {
            MessageBox.Show("You checked: " + item);
        }
    }
```

3 Run the application, check some items, and then click the button. The checked items are displayed one by one.

Using ComboBoxes

A ComboBox is a one-line TextBox combined with a ListBox. The advantage over a normal TextBox is that the most common choices can be presented without any need to type them in. The advantage over a ListBox is that a ComboBox takes less space. ComboBoxes also allow the user to type in a choice that is not on the list. The example here is a person's title. Usually this is one of a few common options: Mr, Mrs, Miss etc. The range of possibilities though is much greater, including rarities like Princess or President. The ComboBox is an ideal solution.

Placing a ComboBox

You can retrieve the value the user has chosen by inspecting the Text property of the ComboBox, or the SelectedItem if you need more than the string value.

Place a ComboBox on a form. The other labels and TextBoxes on the form shown are not essential to run the example.

Open the Load event for the form and write code to fill the ComboBox. Then set the SelectedIndex to your preferred default. For example:

```
this.comboBox1.Items.Add("Mr");
this.comboBox1.Items.Add("Mrs");
comboBox1.SelectedIndex = 0;
```

If you don't want the user choosing a value not on the list, choose DropDownList.

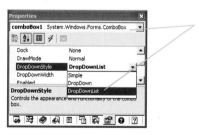

Try setting the DropDownStyle property to different values and then running the application. Dropdown is the default.

To use Simple Combo you need to increase the height of the ComboBox.

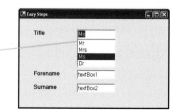

The OpenFileDialog Control

Many Windows applications need to load or save files on disk. That could involve writing a lot of code, but fortunately Visual C# makes it easy to use the standard Windows dialog for this.

Controls like OpenFileDialog and SaveFileDialog are similar to other controls, in that you use them by selecting an icon in the Toolbox and placing it on a form. They are different, though, because they appear in a space below the form in the Designer, and are invisible when the application runs. However you can refer to them in code.

Creating a Picture Viewer

When you run the Picture Viewer, you will find that images may be too small or too large to fill the control properly. When you set the SizeMode property to StretchImage, it will be stretched to exactly fill the control. This will also distort the picture, so use it with care. Another option is CenterImage.

1. Place a PictureBox, a button, and an OpenFileDialog Control on a form. For the PictureBox, set the sizemode property to StretchImage.

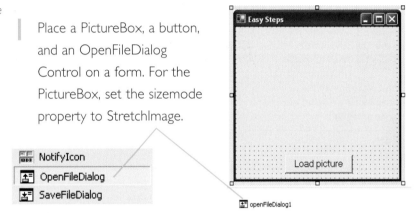

Often you have a choice between setting a property in the Properties window, or elsewhere such as in the Load event for a form. It doesn't matter which you choose. It is easier to type longer properties into the Load event, instead of the small boxes of the Properties window. It also makes it easier to find and edit the code, which is rather hidden away when in the Properties window.

2. Open the form's Load event and add the line:

```
this.openFileDialog1.Filter =
"Pictures|*.bmp;*.ico;*.jpg;*.wmf";
```

Then add the following lines to the button's Click event:

```
if (openFileDialog1.ShowDialog()==DialogResult.OK )
{
  if (openFileDialog1.FileName != string.Empty) {
      this.pictureBox1.Image = new
      Bitmap(openFileDialog1.FileName);
}}
```

Now you can test the application by running it, clicking the button, and finding a bitmap file in the dialog.

There is a group of controls that work in a similar way. Once you understand how the OpenFileDialog Control works, it is easy to use the other dialogs like SaveFileDialog and FontDialog.

More about the OpenFileDialog control

The OpenFileDialog saves the programmer from writing a lot of code to correctly navigate a hard disk or network and find or create files. The Picture Viewer example uses ShowDialog to summon the standard Windows Open dialog.

When it opens, the dialog uses the Filter property to decide which files to show. This helps prevent the user from trying to open the wrong sort of file for your application. When the user clicks Open, the dialog disappears and the name of the chosen file is placed in the Filename property of the OpenFileDialog Control.

The title of the dialog is set by the Title property

The exact appearance of this dialog will vary according to the version of Windows being used. Images may appear as lines in a list, rather than previews as here.

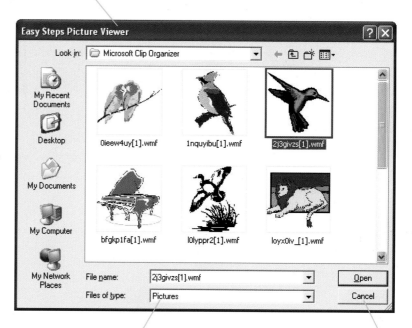

The Picture Viewer works, but if the user chooses a file that is not a picture, it crashes with an error message. See page 118 for how to handle such errors.

The Filter property sets what appears here. This property has two or more parts, separated by the | character. The first is what shows in the "Files of type:" box. The second lists acceptable extensions, divided by a semicolon

If the user clicks Cancel, the Filename property will be empty

Using the timer

The timer is an invisible control like the OpenFileDialog. All it does is fire an event at intervals set by you.

Make the lights flash!

The following example uses two labels, and makes them flash alternately blue and yellow. Controlling the flash is a Timer control, which is an essential part of many animation effects.

You can change the interval property of a timer at runtime. In this example, you could have an option to slow down the flashing or speed it up. You can also move the lights by changing the Top and Left properties of the label control.

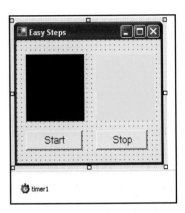

Place a timer, two labels and two buttons on a form. Set the timer's Interval property to 200. This time is in milliseconds. Set one label's BackColor property to Blue, and the other to Yellow.

2 Double-click the timer to open the Tick event. This will run every time the interval elapses. Add this code:

```
if (label1.BackColor == Color.Blue)
{
        label1.BackColor = Color.Yellow;
        label2.BackColor = Color.Blue;
}
else
{
        label1.BackColor = Color.Blue;
        label2.BackColor = Color.Yellow;
}
```

The timer is not as accurate as it first appears. Although the interval is specified in milliseconds, the resolution of the timer is probably 50 times worse than that.

3 For the Start Button's Click event add:
```
timer1.Enabled = true;
```

The Stop Button is the same, but with False.

4 Run the application and see the lights flash!

Using the Tab control

When designing Windows forms, it is easy to run out of space. The Tab control lets you separate groups of controls into different tabs, increasing the space available without much inconvenience to the user.

An example

Place a Tab control on a form. Set its Dock property to Fill. Then click the small button next to TabPages (Collection), to open the TabPage editor.

Once the tabs have been added, you can edit their properties from the form itself, without going back to the TabPage editor. You can also use Add Tab and Remove Tab buttons that appear at the foot of the Properties window when a TabControl is selected.

2 In the TabPage editor, click Add twice, to add two TabPages. Then click OK.

If you place controls on the form, behind the Tab control, they will be visible on all the TabPages. In order to place controls on the form, you will need to temporarily undock the Tab control and move it out of the way.

3 Next, simply lay out the form in the normal way, clicking the TabPage tabs to bring the required section to the front.

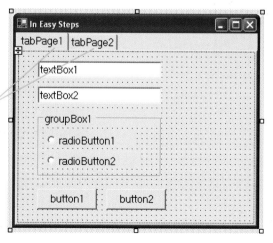

Using the Splitter control

The Splitter control allows the user to resize controls relative to one another at runtime.

An example

1 Place a ListBox control on a form. Set its Dock property to Left. Next, place a Splitter control on the form, and set its Dock property to Left. Finally, place a TextBox control, set its MultiLine property to True and its Dock property to Fill.

 Make sure you add and dock the controls in the right order. If the Splitter is docked right to the edge of the form, instead of on the edge of a control, it will not work.

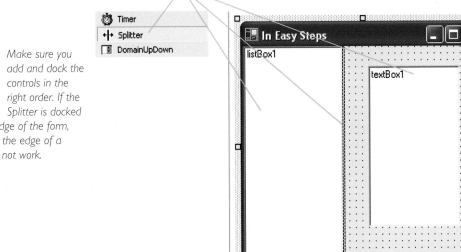

 If you dock the Splitter control to the Top or Bottom, then it becomes a horizontal bar.

2 Run the application, and test the Splitter by clicking on it with the mouse and dragging to left or right. In this example, some items have also been added to the list, and some text to the TextBox.

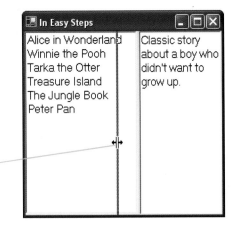

Using the Toolbar and RichTextBox

The RichTextBox is a more powerful version of the TextBox, able to display and edit formatted text. The Toolbar is a row of buttons grouped together on a bar. This example uses both to create a simple word processor.

If you find the RichTextBox going behind the toolbar when you set Dock to fill, try deleting the RichTextBox and adding it back. This can sometimes fix problems with the docking.

1. Place a Toolbar, a RichTextBox and a FontDialogBox on a form. Set the RichTextBox's Dock property to Fill. Set its Font property to a font of your choice.

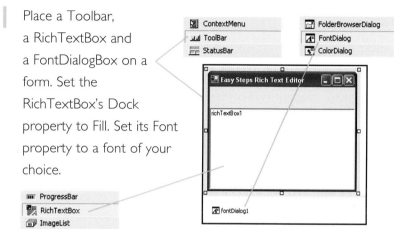

2. Click on the Toolbar, then click the small button in the Properties window to open the Buttons collection. Click Add six times. Set the button Text to Copy, Paste, Bold, Italic, Normal and Font. Then close the button editor.

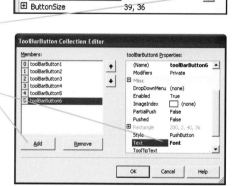

3. Double-click a Toolbar button to open its Click event handler. Toolbar buttons share one Click handler. You can tell which button was clicked by checking the ToolBarButtonClickEventArgs argument. This argument has a Button property that references the clicked ToolBarButton. See the next page for a switch statement that determines which button was clicked and runs the appropriate code.

This is not a complete word processor, but it gives an idea of what you can do.

The native format of the RichTextBox is RTF, which is a standard format used by most word processors and also by the Windows clipboard. By adding an OpenFileDialog and a SaveFileDialog you can easily add the capability to load and save documents from disk.

One thing you cannot easily do with the RichTextBox control, in the first version of Visual C#, is print. If you search out .NET resources on the Internet, you can find code for printing a RichTextBox.

4 Add this code to the Toolbar's Click event handler:

```
//Get a valid font
Font f = richTextBox1.SelectionFont;
 if (f == null) {
 f = richTextBox1.Font;
 }
//Take action depending on the text on the Button
 switch (e.Button.Text)  {
 case "Copy":
 richTextBox1.Copy();
 break;
 case "Paste":
 richTextBox1.Paste();
 break;
 case "Bold":
 richTextBox1.SelectionFont = new Font(f,
     FontStyle.Bold);
 break;
 case "Italic":
 richTextBox1.SelectionFont = new Font(f,
     FontStyle.Italic);
 break;
 case "Normal":
 richTextBox1.SelectionFont = new Font(f,
     FontStyle.Regular);
 break;
 case "Font":
 if (fontDialog1.ShowDialog() == DialogResult.OK)  {
 richTextBox1.SelectionFont  = fontDialog1.Font;
 }
 break;
 }
```

5 Run the application. To make text bold or italic, select it and press the Bold or Italic button. You can also Copy and Paste, even with images.

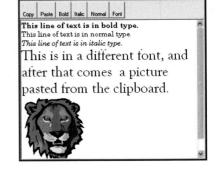

Using the MonthCalendar control

Many C# applications deal with dates. Two controls make it easy to select and display dates. The MonthCalendar displays a month to view, with buttons for moving to other months. The DateTimePicker is a drop-down MonthCalendar, ideal for saving space on forms where you need to display a single date. The MonthCalendar lets you select a range of dates. You can retrieve the start date from the SelectionStart property, and the end date from the SelectionEnd property.

Place a MonthCalendar and a TextBox on a form. Set the TextBox's Multiline property to True, and Dock to Bottom.

Double-click the MonthCalendar to open its DateChanged event handler. Add this code:

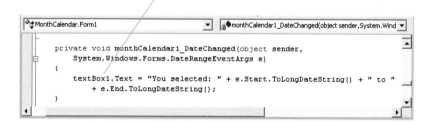

```csharp
private void monthCalendar1_DateChanged(object sender,
    System.Windows.Forms.DateRangeEventArgs e)
{
    textBox1.Text = "You selected: " + e.Start.ToLongDateString() + " to "
        + e.End.ToLongDateString();
}
```

Run the application, and select a range of dates to try it out. Click the month name to drop-down a list of months. The dates selected appear in the TextBox.

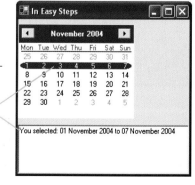

Setting tab order

Not all users like to use the mouse. Therefore you should allow keyboard alternatives wherever possible. One way is by keyboard shortcuts for buttons and menu options. Another factor is that users expect to be able to move the focus from one control to another by pressing Tab. You need to ensure that the focus moves in a logical order when Tab is pressed. The solution is to set the TabIndex property.

Setting the tab order can be confusing, because when you change the TabIndex of one control, Visual Studio will alter other TabIndex properties automatically. The tab order will remain the same though, apart from the actual control you are editing.

How to set the tab order

1. Place several controls on a form, or open a form you have been working on. Then, from the View menu, choose Tab Order. Small tabs appear on each control, indicating the current tab order.

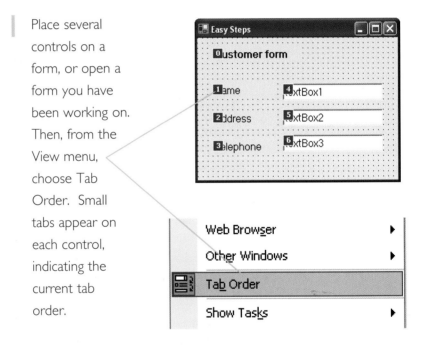

2. Carefully click on each control in turn, in the order you want the Tab order to be. If you make a mistake, you can start again once you have clicked all the controls.

Some other controls

There are several other controls in the standard Toolbox:

The **LinkLabel** is a label that can contain hyperlinks. Use it to give a Web look to a Windows application

The **MainMenu** and **ContextMenu** controls are covered on pages 96-100. They are used for adding a custom menu to a form

A powerful control, the **DataGrid** is covered on pages 159-164. It is mainly for database applications

Before adding the scrollbar to a project, check to see if the object for which you want the scrollbar already has a Scrollbars property. Some objects appear with a scrollbar by default. These built-in scrollbars are much easier to work with than the separate scrollbar controls.

HScrollBar and **VScrollBar** are used for creating custom scrollbars. The **TrackBar** is similar, but with a different look and feel

The **DomainUpDown** for strings lets the user click through a collection of strings

The **NumericUpDown** control lets the user change a number by clicking on small arrows

The **ProgressBar** is for displaying the progress of a long operation

Using Anchor and Dock properties

Users like to be able to resize forms, for example to view more of the text in a textbox without scrolling. It is important to control what happens when a form is resized. Visual C# makes this easy with the Anchor and Dock properties. Anchor can be set to any combination of Top, Bottom, Left and Right. The Anchor property means "stay at the same distance from these edges when the form is resized". Dock means "fill the area right up to the specified edge". Here are some possibilities:

Typically, you will want fixed-size controls like buttons to be anchored to a corner, whereas controls that benefit from a larger size, such as TextBoxes or ListBoxes, will be anchored so they stretch as the form is resized.

- If you anchor a control to a corner, then it remains the same size and stays the same distance from that corner when the form is resized. The default is Top Left

- If you anchor a control to an edge, then it remains the same size and distance from that edge, but will move along the edge when the edge itself is resized

- If you anchor a control to three edges, it will stretch as the control is resized, so it remains the same distance from all three edges

- If you anchor a control to all four edges, then the control will stretch so that its distance from each edge remains the same as the form is resized. This way you can set a control to fill a form completely

For complex forms, use panels to contain your other controls. The controls can be anchored to the panel, and the panel anchored to the form, enabling full control over resizing. Another possibility is to write code for the SizeChanged event, if the Anchor property does not give enough flexibility.

- If you want a control to fill one side of a form right to the edge, or to fill a form completely, use the Dock property instead of Anchor

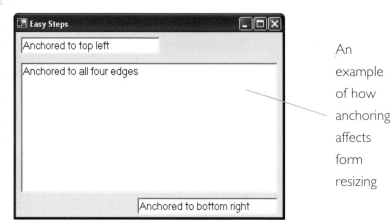

An example of how anchoring affects form resizing

C# Language Essentials

Visual C# lets you do a lot of your work visually but you still need to write code that controls the visual components. Snippets of C# have already appeared in Chapters One and Two. You'll now learn to write programs of your own.

Covers

Chapter Three

Start at the beginning

Programs are a series of instructions that tell the computer what to do. Although programs can be complex, each individual instruction is generally simple. The computer starts at the beginning and works through line by line until it gets to the end. Here are some of the essential elements in C#:

The best way to learn how to program is by doing it. Visual C# is a safe environment in which to try things out and learn from your mistakes.

Statement

This is an instruction that directs the computer how to run your program. For example, the **if** statement means do something if a condition is true.

Variables

These are words that store a value. For example, the line:

```
myvar = "Visual C#";
```

stores a string of characters in a variable called myvar.

Operators

Don't confuse assignment (=) with testing for equality (==). Many languages use the same symbol for both, but C# does not.

A word or symbol that indicates an operation to be performed. Examples are the arithmetical operators, like "+", "–" and "=". To avoid confusion with a letter, the symbol used for multiplication is the asterisk: "*". Division is expressed by the forward-sloping slash character: "/". The operator for "equals" is ==, "or" is |, and for "not equals" it is !=.

Objects and Classes

Objects can be visible, like forms or buttons, or invisible, like the Windows clipboard. You can also create custom objects. In C#, any element can be treated as an object. The code that defines an object is called a Class.

C# is called an object-oriented programming language, because every element is an object or can be treated as one.

Properties

Properties are the characteristics of an object.

Methods

Methods are actions an object can perform. For example, Forms have a Hide method which makes the form invisible. Some methods return a value.

Parameters

Values passed to methods are called parameters or arguments. Some properties take parameters as well.

An example program

Here is a simple program with an explanation of its parts:

All those curly
brackets look
confusing when
you first start
programming.
See the next page for an
explanation.

1 Place a label, a textbox and a
button on a form. Set the text
properties as shown. Then
double-click the button to
open the code editor for the
Click event.

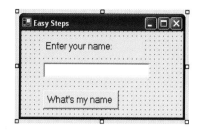

2 Type in the code as shown below, beginning with the line starting
"myvar..." and ending with the last indented curly bracket. The
rest of the code is generated automatically. You are typing into a
"private void" which means a subroutine that is only accessible
from this form (private).

In C#, you
declare a variable
by stating its type,
and then the
variable name.
The myvar variable is a string, so:
string myvar;

This line tells C# that we are going to use a
variable called myvar to hold a string value

What about all
that other code
Visual C#
generates? See
page 54 for a
quick tour.

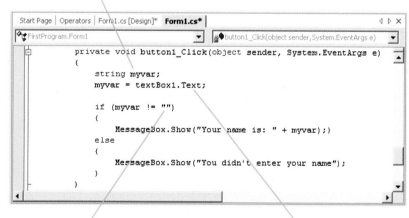

```
Start Page | Operators | Form1.cs [Design]* | Form1.cs* |                    ◁ ▷ ×
FirstProgram.Form1                        ▼    button1_Click(object sender,System.EventArgs e)  ▼
            private void button1_Click(object sender, System.EventArgs e)
            {
                string myvar;
                myvar = textBox1.Text;

                if (myvar != "")
                {
                    MessageBox.Show("Your name is: " + myvar);}
                else
                {
                    MessageBox.Show("You didn't enter your name");
                }
            }
```

Next, C# compares the string in myvar
to an empty string. If it is not empty, a
message appears showing the value,
otherwise a message informs the user
that no text has been entered. An
empty string is shown as """

This line is executed right
to left. First, C# obtains
the Text property of
textBox1. The resulting
string is stored in the
myvar variable

The parts of a C# file

A C# file has several distinct parts. Here are the main ones described in brief. They are explained in more detail later.

Using statements

At the top of most C# files are one or more statements beginning **using**. These statements tell the compiler where to look for classes you refer to later on. Using statements do not run, and they are always optional. They simply save some typing.

Namespace declaration

Most C# files have a **namespace** declaration, followed by a block marked by curly bracket. Namespaces are a way of organizing code so the compiler can find the classes you define.

Comments

Any line of code that begins with two or more forward slashes is a comment. Some comments have special meaning, enabling C# to document your code automatically.

Not all C# files define a class. Others may define interfaces or custom type.

Class statement

A C# file can contain one or more classes, though one class per file is most common. The class statement introduces a new class, marked again by curly brackets.

Class-level variables

As described on the previous page, variables declared within the class but outside any method or property are visible throughout the class, and optionally outside it as well.

Method declarations

Most of the additional code in a C# file defines methods and properties. These are the "member functions" that specify the functionality of the class.

Directives

Statements beginning # are instructions to the compiler, known as preprocessor directives.

The code Visual C# generates is needed for your programs to run. If you amend it, it can be hard to fix, so be cautious about changing or deleting anything you didn't actually type.

Generated code

Some code generated by the Visual C# form designer is marked as such and you are normally expected to leave it alone. However, it is still ordinary C# code.

Introducing data types

Along with scope, another important characteristic of a variable is its type. This determines what kind of information (data) a variable can hold.

Anything within double quotation marks is a string. For example, "123" is a string and not a number. The contents of text boxes are strings as well.

For example, a string variable stores a string of characters. This is useful for things like names and addresses, but is of no use for mathematical calculations. If you want to store numbers and perform calculations, you need a numeric variable like an integer.

There is also a general-purpose type called an *Object*. Objects hold data of any type. However, that does not mean you can simply declare every variable as an object and forget about types. For example, even if you have two objects both containing numbers, C# will not be able to add them together directly. You have to tell the compiler to treat them as numbers, using what is called a cast (see page 74). If you know the variables will be used only to store numbers, it is easier and faster to declare them as the correct type in the first place. As shown below, you declare a variable by entering the type followed by the variable name.

In C# any data type can be treated as an object. That means casting a variable to an object always succeeds.

Even object types will not let you do the impossible. For example, you cannot cast a string to a number. If you try, C# will report an "Invalid cast" exception. There are specific functions that can convert strings to numbers and vice versa, but this is conversion, rather than casting.

Built-in and custom types

C# has a few basic types, such as int, bool, char and float. These accept literal values, so you can type things like:

```
int someNumber;
someNumber = 4;
```

More complex types are defined in custom classes, or as part of the .NET Framework class library. You can also have arrays and collections, which are in effect a set of variables all of the same type.

Exploring data types

C# has thirteen simple data types as well as string and object:

byte	Integer 0 to 255
sbyte	Integer -127 to 128
short	Integer -32768 to 32767
ushort	Integer 0 to 65535
int	Integer -2147483648 to 2147483647
uint	Integer 0 to 4294967295
long	Integer -9223372036854775808 to 9223372036854775807
ulong	Integer 0 to 18446744073709551615
char	Like ushort but corresponds to an unicode character
float	Floating point $1.5 \times 10{-45}$ to 3.4×1038 with a precision of 7 digits
double	Floating point $5.0 \times 10{-324}$ to 1.7×10308 with a precision of 15-16 digits
bool	True or false
decimal	Currency value $1.0 \times 10{-28}$ to about 7.9×1028 with 28-29 significant digits
string	String of any length (limited by memory)
object	Any type

Although there is a wide range of types, they fall into a few groups. There are nine integer types, including char which represents a single character. Computers store characters as numbers, which is why the character type is really just a number. Then there are two floating point types, the special decimal type for working with money values, bool for yes/no values, and the string which stores any number of characters.

Doing sums

This example program is a calculator. You type in two numbers, and the program adds, subtracts, divides or multiplies the numbers depending on which button you click. To make it work, two data types are needed. The input (what the user types) and the output (what is displayed on the screen) are strings, while the calculations use floating point numbers. If you used integer types, the calculator would only work with whole numbers.

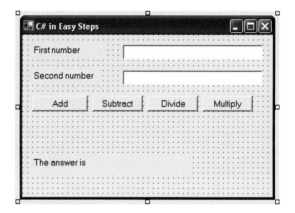

Start a new application with a blank form. Place labels, text boxes and buttons on the form as shown.

In this style of naming, the prefix reminds you of what kind of object it is, txt for a TextBox, btn for a Button and so on.

2 Display the Properties window (F4), select each of the active controls on the form, and edit its Name property. Name the controls as follows:

txtFirstNumber
txtSecondNumber
btnAdd
btnSubtract
btnDivide
btnMultiply
lbResult

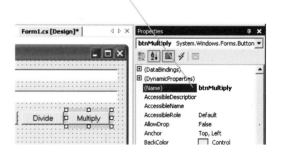

3 Now double-click the Add button and enter the code shown in the Click event handler. Notice that you have to convert from string to float to do the calculation, and then convert the result back to string in order to display it. C# has two handy methods for this. The basic types have a static Parse method that takes a string and converts it to that type, and all objects in the .NET Framework have a ToString() method that converts their value to a string.

You'll notice that the calculation code comes within a block beginning with "try". The reason for this is to catch any errors, for example if nothing is typed into the textboxes. This is a technique called exception handling, explained on page 118.

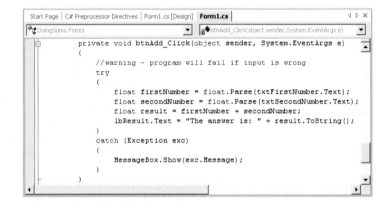

```
private void btnAdd_Click(object sender, System.EventArgs e)
{
    //warning - program will fail if input is wrong
    try
    {
        float firstNumber = float.Parse(txtFirstNumber.Text);
        float secondNumber = float.Parse(txtSecondNumber.Text);
        float result = firstNumber + secondNumber;
        lbResult.Text = "The answer is: " + result.ToString();
    }
    catch (Exception exc)
    {
        MessageBox.Show(exc.Message);
    }
}
```

You can use copy and paste to save typing such similar code. However, there is an even better way to do it, which is to create a separate method.

4 Type similar code for the other buttons. The only difference will be in the line that calculates the result. Replace the "+" in step 3 with:

–	for Subtract
/	for Divide
*	for Multiply

If you need to handle larger numbers, use a double instead of a float.

Then run the program to try it out. But make sure you enter numbers in the text boxes before clicking the buttons, otherwise the program will fail. Very large numbers or entering text that is not a number will also make it fail. For example, if you enter a word instead of a number you get the message "Input string was not in a correct format." This occurs because C# cannot convert the string to a float.

Curly brackets and semicolons

All programming languages based on C, including C# and Java, seem to be full of curly brackets and semicolons. This is because they mark out the building blocks of a program. Programs are executed line by line, so C# needs to know where each line ends. It's inconvenient to use an actual line break, since some lines of code are very long, and code is much easier to read if the lines on the page (or in the code editor) are short. Therefore, C# treats everything as on the same line until it meets a semicolon.

Another handy feature is that white space and tab characters are ignored, as long as there is at least one space between each word. That means you can freely space out your code to make it easier to read.

Whereas semicolons indicate the end of a line, curly brackets surround a block of lines that must be read together. You can get blocks of code within other blocks of code, so the brackets are frequently nested. For example, curly brackets mark out the beginning and end of a class, the beginning and end of a function, and the beginning and end of code that runs after if, when the condition is true.

The if statement is a good example. Without curly brackets, each if statement only enables a single line:

```
if (somevar = 2)
    somevar = 1;
    anothervar = 2;
```

Despite the indentation, the second line, "anothervar = 2", always runs. It is outside the control of "if". If you want both lines to depend on the outcome of the if statement, use curly brackets:

```
if (somevar = 2)
{
    somevar = 1;
    anothervar = 2;
}
```

Now both lines of code are treated as a single block.

For every opening bracket, whether curly, round or square, there is always a closing bracket. The only exception is if they appear within quotes as a passive string of text.

Visual C# has a handy Format feature that lines up and indents all your curly brackets. To use it, highlight the code you want to format, and choose Edit > Advanced > Format selection.

To avoid confusion, always use curly brackets with if, unless the entire statement is on one line.

Functions and parameters

Some programming languages, like Visual Basic, distinguish between functions and subroutines (or procedures). Functions return a value, while procedures do not. In C#, both are treated as functions. To accommodate the fact that not all functions return a value, there is a special return value called "void". Therefore, the equivalent of a subroutine in C# is a function returning void.

Writing a custom function in C# starts off much like declaring a variable. You write the data type returned by the function, and then the function name. Here's an example:

```
string Hello()
{
    return "Hello";
}
```

There's no semicolon after the line which declares the function. If you forget, and type a semicolon, C# will raise an error on compilation.

The curly brackets mark out where the function code begins and ends. You'll also notice a pair of round brackets after the function name. These contain any values passed to the function. In this case, there are none, but C# still requires the brackets.

Passing parameters is essential for many functions. For example, here is a function that counts the characters in a word:

```
int CountLetters(string theWord)
{
    return theWord.Length;
}
```

You will often see additional words before the data type, such as public static. These modify where you can use the function and how it behaves. See page 62.

You can have more than one parameter, in which case they are separated by commas:

```
int CountLetters(string theWord,bool includeSpaces)
```

Functions or methods?

C# is object-oriented, so all functions actually belong to a class (see page 77). This means they are often called "methods" rather than functions. Although all methods are in classes, they do not always require an object to be declared. If the method is declared static, it behaves like a function in a non object-oriented language. See page 89.

Giving variables a value

Much programming involves assigning values to variables and reading them back later. Here are the essential facts about assigning values to variables.

Initial values

When you assign a value to a variable passed as a parameter, the value may not stick when the routine ends. It depends on whether it is passed by reference or by value – see page 72.

When you declare a variable in C#, it has no initial value. If you refer to the value of a local variable before one has been assigned, C# will not compile the code:

```
int y;
if (y ==0) {}; // will not compile
```

You can give a value to a variable in a couple of different ways. In the case of simple types, you can assign a literal value, such as a number or string that you type directly:

```
int y;
string s;
y = 2;
s = "Easy Steps";
```

You can also do this in the same line as the variable is declared:

```
int y = 2;
```

The type name following the new keyword always ends with either round or square brackets. The round brackets remind you that you are calling a constructor (see page 78). Square brackets are for an array (see page 69).

Non-local variables behave slightly differently. These receive a default value according to their type (see below).

The new keyword

Instead of assigning a literal value, another approach is to use the new keyword. This means "get me a new instance of this type". The new keyword works with both simple types and custom classes. For example:

```
int y = new int();
```

Default values

If a simple type (listed on page 56) has been created with new, but has not otherwise been assigned a value, it has a default value. This is zero for numeric types, false for bool, and an empty string for strings. Objects and other reference types (see page 72) have a default value of null until **new** is used. Once created, the initial value depends on the custom class which defines the object.

Variables and scope

In the example on page 52, a variable called myvar was used to store a string of characters. It is called a variable because its contents can change during the course of a program.

Variables have some important characteristics. One of them is called scope or visibility. This determines which parts of a program are able to inspect or change the value of the variable.

How visible should your variables be? The answer is, as little as possible. It may seem handy to have lots of public or global variables, but it makes errors more likely as well.

The myvar variable was declared in a method. Variables like this, declared in a method are visible only within that routine. In fact, if they are declared within a block of code, they are only visible within that block.

Variables can also be declared at the class level in a form or code module. These variables usually come at the beginning of a class, after the class statement and before any method declarations. If you declare these private, then only other routines in that class can use them. If you declare them public they are visible anywhere. Variables declared without any specific scope are private by default.

Other scope specifiers such as protected and internal will be explained later in the book.

This is a public variable visible throughout the project

This is a private variable visible to all routines in this form or module

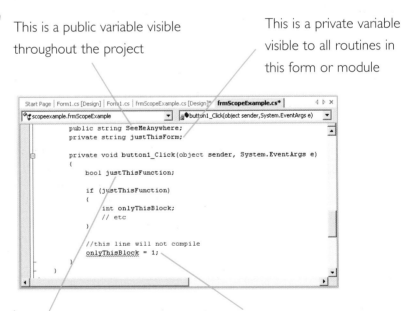

This is a local variable visible only in the button1_Click event handler

This line will not compile since the variable is out of scope. It is only valid within the if block

Using if... else...

C#'s **if** statement lets you add intelligence to your programs, by doing one thing or another depending on a condition you set.

Putting it to work

To open the code editor at the right point, you must double-click the background of the form itself, not the label.

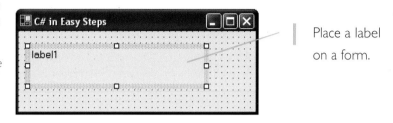

Place a label on a form.

2 Double-click the form to open the code editor at the form load event. This code will run when the application starts.

This code uses some handy .NET Framework functions. Now contains the current date and time. DayOfWeek is an enumeration representing the day. With code completion in Visual C#, it is easy to type this kind of code without having to remember any special names.

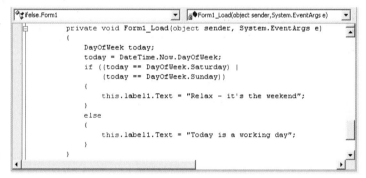

```
private void Form1_Load(object sender, System.EventArgs e)
{
    DayOfWeek today;
    today = DateTime.Now.DayOfWeek;
    if ((today == DayOfWeek.Saturday) |
        (today == DayOfWeek.Sunday))
    {
        this.label1.Text = "Relax - it's the weekend";
    }
    else
    {
        this.label1.Text = "Today is a working day";
    }
}
```

3 Enter this code as shown and then run the program.

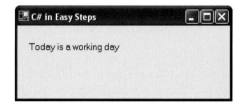

Notice that in C# the **if** condition must be enclosed with round brackets. The **else** part is optional. Another variation is **if ... else if ... else**, which lets you have a series of blocks with different conditions.

Using do and while

Many programs need to loop round the same code a number of times. The **while** statement means "do the following block of code in a loop while this condition is true." The **do** statement is the same, except that the test comes at the end of the loop, so the loop always runs at least once.

An example

1 Place a button on a form.

2 Double-click the button and enter the following code for the Click event handler:

```
DialogResult i;
do
{
i = MessageBox.Show("Choose yes to exit, No to
continue","Easy Steps",MessageBoxButtons.YesNo);
} while (i != DialogResult.Yes);
```

You can also place the condition at the beginning of the loop, in the form while (condition). In this case, the loop may never run at all, if the condition is false.

3 Run the application and click the button. A dialog appears. If you click Yes the dialog closes, but if you click No it closes and immediately reappears.

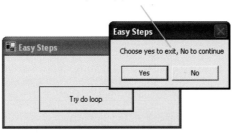

More advanced code can use a feature called multi-threading to run long-running code in a loop while still enabling the user to cancel or quit if necessary.

What if you make a mistake, and your code runs in a loop with no exit? Switch to Visual Studio, and choose Debug > Stop debugging to end the application. However, this is a bad mistake in a real application. The user will have to use the Task Manager to end the application.

You can exit a loop in code with the **break** statement. Another handy statement is **continue**, which exits the current iteration and moves on to the next one.

Using for loops

The for... loop is similar to do..., except that it uses a variable that tells the code how many times the loop has been executed.

A for... example

This application calculates the annual interest on a sum of money entered by the user.

The for... loop uses a counter variable so that the correct number of loops is performed. In the example this is called i. Be very cautious about assigning a value to this variable inside the loop, otherwise you will not get the expected number of iterations. Most programmers regard it as bad practise to assign a value to the loop counter.

1 Place a label, text box, button and list box on a form as shown.

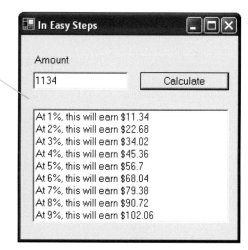

2 Double-click the button and type in this code for the Click event (to use the application, enter a number into the text box and then click the button):

You can nest loops inside one another, and combine them with if...else and other blocks. This is a powerful technique, but can get confusing if there are too many levels.

```
decimal amount;
listBox1.Items.Clear();

try
{
amount = decimal.Parse(textBox1.Text);
  for (int i=1;i<10;i++)
      {
      decimal earnings = amount * i/100;
      listBox1.Items.Add("At " + i.ToString() + "%,
      this will earn $"
      + earnings.ToString());
      }
}
catch (Exception exc)
{
MessageBox.Show(exc.Message);
}
```

Unpacking the for statement

The for statement has three parts, separated by semicolons.

The first part states the variable to be used. This might be already declared, or it can be declared within the statement itself. It's normally best to declare it in the statement, so then you can be sure that it is used solely as a counter. The scope of the variable is then limited to the block of code that forms the loop, which is also good. It must be an integer variable.

Next comes the condition part. This is like an "if" condition for the loop. If it is true, the loop continues, otherwise it stops and the code following the loop is executed. A common mistake is called an "off by one" error. For example, a casual glance at the interest calculator might make you think the loop runs ten times. In fact it runs nine times, because the counter starts at 1 and continues up to and including 9.

The third part of the statement is the change part. The expression "++" means increment by one; it is shorthand for:

```
i = i + 1;
```

You could have a more complex change part, although ++ (or the negative equivalent --) are by far the most common. For example, you could use:

```
i = i + 2;
```

to work with just odd or just even numbers. Naturally, you then get half as many iterations.

In programming, there are usually many different ways to get the output you want. Good code is both efficient and clear, so that when you or someone else looks at it later, it will be easy to figure out how it works.

If you want 20 tests using even numbers, have the **for** statement express the number of tests you want, like this:

```
for (int i = 1; i<=20; i++)
```

To get the even numbers, just work with i*2 in the loop. On the other hand, if you want to test every even number up to 100, this would be more natural:

```
for (int i = 2; i<=100; i = i + 2)
```

This way, the for statement expresses the intention.

Using switch

If... Then is a good way to create branches in your code, but can be awkward when there are lots of possible branches. C# has the switch statement, which let you run different code depending on the value of a test variable.

A switch example

 In this example, note that the line beginning with two slashes is a comment which does nothing at runtime. Comments are a useful way to make programs easier to read.

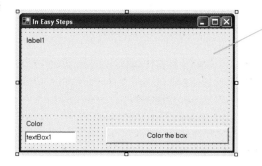

Place two labels, a text box and a button on a form as shown.

2 Double-click the button and enter the following code:

 ToUpper() and Trim() are useful methods to prevent confusion when the user types in mixed case or leaves leading or trailing spaces.

```
string theColor = textBox1.Text.Trim().ToUpper();
label1.Text = theColor;
switch (theColor)
{
        case "RED":
        label1.BackColor = Color.Red;
        break;
        case "BLUE":
        label1.BackColor = Color.Blue;
        break;
        //etc ... add other colors
        default:
        label1.BackColor = Color.White;
        label1.Text = "Unknown color";
        break;
}
```

 A better way to choose colors in Visual C# is to use the ColorDialog control. This example is just to show how switch works.

3 Run the application, type a color into the text box, and click the button.

More about the switch expression

The expression used in the switch statement can be an integer, a string, or a function that returns an integer or string. It is also fine to use an enumerated type (see page 71), which makes for particularly clear code:

To run this code you need to define the MusicType enum elsewhere. See page 71 for details.

```
MusicType theType;
//code to get the MusicType
    switch (theType)
    {
    case MusicType.classical:
    break;
    case MusicType.country:
    break;
    //etc
    }
```

Falling through and multiple cases

Every case statement must end with a jump statement that tells C# where to go next. Normally this is **break**, which means jump to the next statement after the switch block. You can also use **goto case** or **goto default**, in order to jump to another case statement. This means that you cannot inadvertently fall through from one case block to the next. However, you can stack several case statements so that a block of code applies to all of them:

```
case "RED":
case "SCARLET":
//code here is for both RED and SCARLET
```

switch vs if

To get the best of both worlds, use a function which returns an enum as the switch expression. Then your function can use whatever logic is needed to return the right enum value for your switch block.

The **switch** statement is more suitable than **if** when you have a list of different cases. However, **if** is more flexible since you are not restricted to a single expression:

```
if (mystringvar=="BLUE") {
}
else if (myintvar == 23) {
}
//etc
```

Arrays: dealing with a set of values

By now you will have got used to the idea of variables, which let you store values while your program is running.

Once you have declared an array, be careful not to try to access elements that do not exist. In this example, if you referred to MonthlySales(20) C# would report a "Index was outside the bounds" error.

The M suffix after a number tells C# to treat it as a decimal value.

Sometimes it is convenient to deal with a set of values. For example, you might want to work on the monthly sales figures for a year. Rather than having 12 variables called JanSales, FebSales etc, it would be better to have a single array with 12 elements. Then you can refer to MonthlySales[0], MonthlySales[1] instead. Here is an example:

```
decimal[] MonthlySales = new decimal[12];
decimal TotalSales;
MonthlySales[0] = 2213.52M;
MonthlySales[1] = 3215.63M;
MonthlySales[2] = 2314.52M;
//etc
```

A big advantage of arrays is that you can process them in a loop. For instance, the following routine goes on to work out total sales for the year:

C# array elements always start at zero. That means the last element of a 12-element array is numbered 11. But when you instantiate an array, you specify the number of elements. So in this example, the array is instantiated as decimal[12], with the elements numbered 0 to 11.

```
for (int  i= 0; i < 12; i++)
    {
    TotalSales = TotalSales + MonthlySales[i];
    }

label1.Text = "Total sales: $" + TotalSales.ToString();
```

Multiple dimensions

Arrays can have more than one dimension. For example, you could store sales for two shops in one array:

```
decimal[,] MonthlySales = new decimal[12,2];
decimal TotalSales = 0;
MonthlySales[0,0] = 2213.52M; // first shop
MonthlySales[0,1] = 3215.63M; // second shop
//etc
```

Arrays of objects

Arrays can be of any type. However, C# also has an ArrayList type which is easier to work with than a simple array. For example, its size grows and shrinks on demand. See page 82.

Using structs

Sometimes you need to store more than one value in a variable. For example, if your application deals with customers, you might want to store a name, address and telephone number for each customer. One approach would be to have three variables, CustName, CustAddress and CustTel. A better way is to have a Customer variable divided into fields, so you can refer to Customer.Name, Customer.Address and Customer.Telephone. In C# you would normally use a class for this (see page 77), but you can also use a multi-field variable called a struct.

A struct example

This application uses a Customer struct. Here is the definition:

```
struct Customer
{
public string name;
public string address;
public string telephone;
}
```

Although it is used for this simple example, it is usually best not to define types within a file that also defines a form, unless it is solely for use within that form. You can either use a separate file for each type, or define a series of related types in a single file.

1 Right-click a form and choose view code. At the bottom of the file, just before the final curly bracket, enter the definition as shown above.

2 Then select the Design tab, add a button to the form, and double-click to open the click event handler. Add some code to use the struct:

```
Customer mycust;
mycust.name = "Helen Baker";
mycust.address = "1 The Street";
mycust.telephone = "123456789";
MessageBox.Show(mycust.name + ", " +
mycust.address);
```

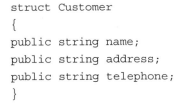

Although you do not have to use new with structs, it is allowed and often makes for clearer code.

What's special about structs?

Structs are value types (see page 72), which means they can be used without the **new** keyword. They support some of the features of classes, such as properties and constructors (provided the constructors take parameters). They can perform better than classes, and are often used for small, lightweight objects. E.g. the .NET Framework defines a Point struct for use in graphics.

Using enums for a range of values

It is common to have a variable that only has a few possible values. For example, a new automobile might be available in one of a few different colors. Perhaps Red, Silver Gray and Navy are on offer, but other colors are not allowed. In C#, you can use an enum type to enforce this:

Enums are a valuable feature of C# for several reasons. First, they help to avoid errors, by restricting the possible values. Second, they let you use Visual C#'s auto-complete when typing code. Third, they use integer types internally, which is faster and uses less memory than alternatives like strings or objects.

Create a new Windows application, add a button to the form, and double-click the button to open the code editor. At the bottom of the file, just before the final curly bracket, enter the definitions for automobile and autoColor. Then add the code for the click event handler. Run the application to test your code.

```
private void button1_Click(object sender, System.EventArgs e)
{
    automobile myauto = new automobile();
    myauto.color = autoColor.Navy;
    myauto.price = 15000.00M;
    MessageBox.Show("My auto is : " + myauto.color.ToString());
}


enum autoColor
{
    Red,
    SilverGray,
    Navy
}

struct automobile
{
    public autoColor color;
    public decimal price;
}
```

More about enums

C# stores enum values as integers. By default it is an int type, but you can specify another integer type. You can also specify which integer C# uses for each value:

```
enum autoColor: byte
{
    Red = 1,
    SilverGray = 2,
    Navy =3
}
```

As in the example, ToString() returns the name of the value, which can be useful.

Understanding reference types

In the real world, houses and offices come in many different sizes, but each one has an address that can be written on an envelope. The same applies to a computer's memory, where every variable and object, large or small, has an address that represents its location.

If you want to write a new value to a variable that has been passed as a parameter, make sure you understand the difference between value and reference parameters.

When you pass a variable as a parameter to a method or function, there is a choice to be made. You can copy the value of the variable and send the copy, or you can send the address of the variable itself. If the receiving function only reads the variable, it makes no difference to the result, but does impact performance and memory usage. If the receiving function changes the variable, it makes a big difference, since if it changed a copy, the changes will be lost once the receiving function completes. By default, parameters in C# are passed by value. You can force a parameter to be passed by reference with the **ref** modifier. The **out** modifier is similar to "ref", but with "out" you do not need to initialize the variable.

Since objects are reference types, you can pass large objects to functions and methods without worrying about memory usage. Only the address of the object is actually passed to the called function.

C# has **value** types and **reference** types. Value types are usually stored in a fast, local area of memory called the stack. When they are passed as a parameter, the computer makes a copy of the value. Reference types are stored in a large, general-purpose area of memory called the heap. In C#, only simple types (see page 56) and structs are value types. Other objects are reference types. Value types are faster, so are ideal for algorithms that read and write variables thousands of times over in a loop. Reference types generally make more efficient use of memory, since only a single address is passed when they are sent as parameters.

What you need to know

Simple types like int, bool and string are passed by value by default, so any changes made will not be seen by the calling function. The reason is that the function receives a copy of the value.

Even object variables are passed by value. That means you are passing a copy of the variable whose value is the address of the object. If the called function assigns a new object to the variable, the calling function will not see it unless the parameter is modified with ref or out.

If you pass an object or other reference type to a function, any changes made to the object will be seen by the calling function. The reason is that only one object exists in memory, and the value of the variable simply contains the address of the object.

You can always force a variable to be passed by reference, using the **ref** modifier, or **out** if you do not want to initialize it first.

Working with parameters

This example demonstrates the use of three parameter types.

1   Create a new Windows application, and add three labels and a button to the form.

2   Double-click the button to open its Click event handler. Before entering code for the button click, type in the definition for a new function, SayGoodbye as shown. Then type the code in the click event handler, which calls the new function.

To better understand the difference between ref and out, try removing the initialization from var 2. Visual C# will refuse to compile the code, since ref parameters must be initialized.

```
valueandreference.Form1                                button1_Click(object sender,System.EventArgs e)

            private void button1_Click(object sender, System.EventArgs e)
            {
                string var1 = "Hello";
                string var2 = "Hello";
                string var3; // not initialized

                SayGoodbye(var1,ref var2,out var3);

                this.label1.Text = var1;
                this.label2.Text = var2;
                this.label3.Text = var3;

            }

            private void SayGoodbye(string var1, ref string var2, out string var3)
            {
                var1 = "Goodbye";
                var2 = "Goodbye";
                var3 = "Goodbye";
            }
```

3   Run the application to test it. Notice that the value of the first parameter, passed by value, remains unchanged even though the SayGoodbye function wrote a value to it. The other variables had their values changed, because they were passed by reference.

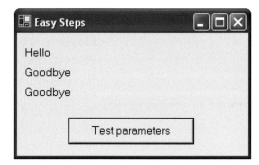

More about casting

All variables in C# have a data type, even if that type is the generic **object**. It is often necessary to treat one type as if it were another. This is called **casting**. It is like converting between types, but it is not really a conversion, since the original data is unchanged. It becomes a conversion if the cast value is then assigned to another variable.

You cannot convert between strings and numeric types with casts. Instead, use the ToString() method to go from a number to a string, and the Parse method to go from a string to a number. For example:
string mystring =
int.Parse("450");

When you cast from one type to another type, one of three things may happen:

1. The cast may succeed, preserving access to all the data in the source variable. For example, if you cast from an integer type to a floating point type, no data is lost (provided that the floating point type is sufficiently large to hold the integer).

2. The cast may succeed, but with loss of data. For example, if you cast a floating point number to an integer, C# will have to truncate it at the decimal point.

3. The cast may fail. For example, you cannot cast a string to a number. Either the compilation will fail with a "cannot convert" message, or at runtime C# will throw an InvalidCastException.

How to perform a cast

You perform a cast by putting the desired data type in round brackets immediately before the variable or expression from which you are casting. For example:

If you want to access a property or method of the target data type after making the cast, you can either assign the cast value to a variable of that type, or else surround the whole cast including the source and target in an additional pair of round brackets. For example:
((int)myfloat).ToString()

```
float myfloat;
int myint;
myfloat = 3.14159F;
myint = (int)myfloat; //this is the cast
MessageBox.Show(myint.ToString());
```

Casting objects

You can cast objects as well as simple types like float and int. When you cast an object, the cast will succeed if the source object type either is, or inherits from, the target object type. If the target is an interface the source must implement that interface. See page 84 for more about inheritance.

Object Essentials

C# is a fully object-oriented language. Although you can build simple applications without learning about objects and classes, it is much easier if you understand the essentials. Learning object-oriented programming also makes it easier to pick up other languages such as Java.

Covers

Chapter Four

A first object

Objects and classes seem complex at first, but they are easy to use, especially in Visual C#. To get started, here is how to add your own custom object to an application:

 You don't have to start a new file to create a class, since you can add a class definition to a Form code file. Most programmers do use separate files for their classes, since it makes code easier to manage.

1 Start a new project and choose Add New Item from the File menu.

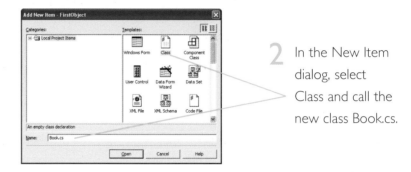

2 In the New Item dialog, select Class and call the new class Book.cs.

 See page 54 for an explanation of the parts of a class.

3 Visual C# opens Book.cs. Find the beginning of the class and type the code as shown. There is also a wizard for creating properties, but it's worth typing out this first one so you understand what the wizard does.

The Book class defines a book, but to use it you need to declare a variable of the type Book, and use the new keyword to create a new Book object.

4 To use your new class, go back to the form in your project, add a button, and create a Click event handler. Add the code below, then run the project.

```
Book MyBook;
MyBook = new Book();
MyBook.Title = Peter Pan";
MessageBox.Show("The title of the book is: " +
MyBook.Title);
```

Classes and objects

The previous example is very simple, but it demonstrates several key facts.

To confuse matters slightly, a class can have static members. These are properties or methods that you call without creating an object. They belong to the class itself.

To begin with, it is vital to understand the difference between a class and an object. A class is like an enhanced data type; it defines a type of object. It is not itself an object. It is like the difference between the architect's plans for a house (the class), and the house itself (the object). It is a good analogy, because just as you can build several houses from one set of plans, you can create multiple objects from a single class.

The code that makes use of the Book class does two important things. First, it declares a variable of the type Book:

```
Book MyBook;
```

Next, it creates an object of the Book type:

```
MyBook = new Book();
```

Creating an object is often called creating an instance of the object, or instantiating the object.

This is like the instruction to the builders to go away and build a house. The computer allocates memory to the new Book object, and the MyBook variable now points at that piece of memory.

Now you can call the properties and methods of the new Book. This object only has one custom property, although it also has some standard properties through the magic of inheritance (see page 84).

The use of classes to define real-world things like books is called Abstraction, because it summarizes the essential characteristics of a book into a few specific properties and methods.

The code for the Title property is somewhat elaborate. The Title itself is stored in a private variable called mTitle. The property definition includes two methods, one called **get** and the other **set**. This means that nobody can access the mTitle variable except through the property code. You could have avoided this by making the mTitle variable Public. That is poor design though. Using the property code means you can ensure the Title is valid, for example disallowing a blank title, or making it always begin with an upper case letter. You can also create read-only properties, by omitting the **set** routine.

Note that the **set** routine refers to an implicit parameter called **value**. The type of this parameter is automatically set to the type of the property itself.

Constructors and destructors

Two critical moments in the lifetime of an object are when it is created and when it is destroyed. The constructor is a special method that gives the programmer control over what happens at creation. There is an equivalent called a destructor, which gets called when the object is destroyed. However, C# programmers use destructors much less than constructors. The reason is that the .NET Framework handles object destruction automatically, through a technique called "garbage collection". Every so often, the .NET runtime checks through memory looking for objects that are no longer in use and freeing their memory. The good thing about this is that you do not normally need to worry about the process. What can be inconvenient is that you do not know when it will happen. Since you don't know when the destructor will be called, it is important not to rely on the code there being run. For beginning programmers, the rule is simple: don't use destructors.

If you use a destructor, remember that you do not know when the code will run. If you want to clean up resources such as closing open files or database connections, use the Dispose method instead (see page 93).

In a C# class, the constructor is a method with the same name as the class:

```
public Book()
{
}
```

It is normally public, but occasionally may have narrower scope. Visual C# automatically creates a constructor when you add a new class using Project > Add class.

The destructor is a method with the name of the class preceded by ~. It does not take a visibility specifier:

```
~Book()
{
}
```

Using a constructor

A constructor is used in most classes. The idea is to define it so that objects are always valid. In the example on the following pages, the Book class is modified so that all Book objects have an Author and a Title. To add flexibility, you can define classes which have more than one constructor, provided each version takes different parameters.

Using Add Field and Add Property

The simple Book class works but does not do much. It's time to enhance it to bring out some of the power of classes and objects.

You do not have to use the Add Field or Add Property wizards. It makes no difference whether you use the wizard or type in the code yourself. Try both techniques and see which you prefer.

All books have an author, so add an author property similar to Title. This time, use the built-in tools to save some typing. Select the Class View (View > Class View) and expand it to find the Book class. Right-click and choose Add Field from the pop-up menu.

If you are adding a property, be sure to make your field private. Otherwise, there is no way to ensure that the field is accessed only through the property.

Complete the Add Field dialog, specifying a private string named mAuthor. Add an appropriate comment. Then click Finish.

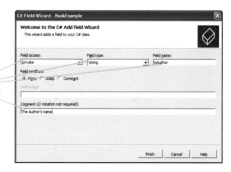

The term Accessors means methods to get or set the value or a property. If you choose get or set alone, you will create a read-only or write-only property.

Right-click the Book class again, and this time choose Add Property. Call the property Author, and specify a public string with get/set Accessors. Then click Finish.

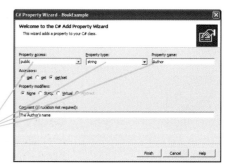

4 In the class view, double-click the Author property. This opens the code with the cursor at the beginning of the property. Edit the code to look like this.

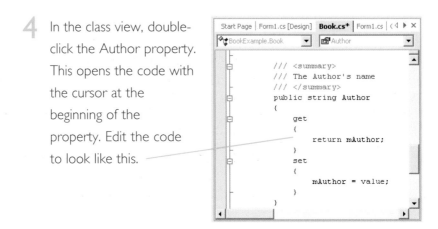

```
/// <summary>
/// The Author's name
/// </summary>
public string Author
{
    get
    {
        return mAuthor;
    }
    set
    {
        mAuthor = value;
    }
}
```

5 We want to ensure that all books have a title and an author. To do so, find the method called simply Book(). This is the constructor (see page 78) and is called whenever a Book object is created. Modify the constructor as shown, adding two parameters as well as the if ... else block.

```
public Book(string author, string title)
{
    if ((author == string.Empty) | (title == string.Empty))
    {
        throw new Exception("Book must have an author and title");
    }
    else
    {
        mAuthor = author;
        mTitle = title;
    }
}
```

The effect of these changes is that Book objects can no longer be created without specifying author and title. If you type:

```
Book mybook = new Book();
```

the code will no longer compile. Instead, type:

```
Book mybook = new Book("William Shakespeare","As you
like it");
```

As a further check, trim the spaces from a string variable using the string's Trim() method. In most cases, if you don't want an empty string you don't want one that is just spaces either.

Finally, if you create a Book object passing an empty string as the Author or Title an exception is thrown. This is a way of adding discipline to your code. In this case, to make it more rigorous, you need to add checks to the property set routines as well, to check for empty strings there.

A list of books

There are several shortcuts for overriding properties and methods. If you type:

```
public override
```

Visual C# will pop-up a list of possibilities. Alternatively, you can right-click a method under Bases and Interfaces, in the Class View, and choose Add > Override.

A common requirement is to present objects in a ListBox. Page 36 shows how to display a list of strings, but in practise this is often not adequate. Typically, when the user selects an entry in a ListBox, your code needs to retrieve further information related to that entry. A powerful technique is to add objects, rather than strings, to the list. Then when the user makes a selection, you can get at all the properties and methods of the selected object.

All objects in C# have a method called ToString(). A ListBox uses this method to determine how to display the object. You can exploit this so that Book objects display in the way you want.

1. Add the following code to Book.cs:

```
public override string ToString()
    {
    return this.Title + " by " + this.Author;
    }
```

It is essential to include the word override if you type this Function. See page 84 for more information about Inheritance.

2. Now add a ListBox to the form in your project, and add a button with the following code in the Click event handler:

```
listBox1.Items.Clear();
listBox1.Items.Add(new Book("Lewis Carroll","Alice in Wonderland"));
listBox1.Items.Add(new Book ("Ian Fleming", "Diamonds are Forever"));
//etc
```

Techniques like this are used in database applications, where the list shows a friendly name, but the programmer deals with a code number that identifies the item in a database.

3. Run the application to see the list. An advantage is that if you retrieve an item from the list, say with the SelectedItem property, you can access all the properties of the Book. For example:

```
Book MyBook = (Book)
    listBox1.SelectedItem;
```

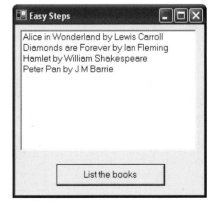

Easy Steps

Alice in Wonderland by Lewis Carroll
Diamonds are Forever by Ian Fleming
Hamlet by William Shakespeare
Peter Pan by J M Barrie

List the books

Working with collections

See page 87 for more information about interfaces.

In the example on the previous page, a number of Book objects were added to the Items property of a ListBox. The Items property is an object of type ObjectCollection. More important, it implements the IList interface, which has many useful properties and methods for working with collections of objects. These include:

Clear: clears the list.

Add: adds an item to the list.

Remove: removes an item from the list.

Item: returns the item at a given place (index) in the list.

Count: returns the number of items in the list.

You can mix objects of different types in an IList, but if you do you will need to take care in order to avoid type mismatch errors.

Items in an IList are of type object. In C#, all classes inherit from object, so that means you can store any type of object in the list. You can even mix objects of different types in the same list.

IList is an interface, which means you cannot instantiate IList objects directly. Instead, you work with classes that implement IList, such as the ArrayList. The following example demonstrates how to store and retrieve items from an ArrayList, working with the Book class as on the previous page.

1 Add a private decimal field mPrice to Book.cs, along with a Price property to get and set the value of mPrice.

```
private decimal mPrice;

public decimal Price
{
    get
    {
        return mPrice;
    }
    set
    {
        mPrice = value;
    }
}
```

If you are continuing to work with the project on page 81, you can delete the listbox and simply change the text of the button. If you start a new project, you can either copy the contents of Book.cs to a new class, or import it using Project > Add Existing item. If you do the latter, change its namespace to that used by the new project.

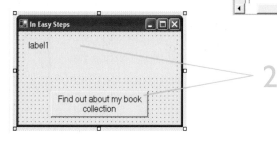

2 On the project's form, have a button and a label as shown.

Like any object variable, MyBooks cannot be used until it is set to refer to an instance of the object. Here, this is done in the Load event using the new keyword.

3 Add a new private member to the form code, of type ArrayList.

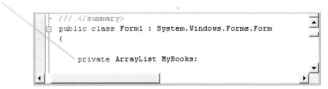

4 Double-click the form to open the Load event handler and add the following code:

```
MyBooks = new ArrayList();
Book aBook;
aBook = new Book("Shakespeare","Hamlet");
aBook.Price = 15.00M;
MyBooks.Add(aBook);
aBook = new Book("Jane Austen","Emma");
aBook.Price = 10.00M;
MyBooks.Add(aBook);
```

Rather than write code like this, it is better to store structured data in a database. See chapter 7 for more information about databases. This is just a quick way to demonstrate use of the ArrayList.

The foreach statement is a great way to iterate (step through) a collection. It does an automatic cast, so that although the ArrayList stores items of type object, you can treat them as Book items within the foreach block.

5 Now add the following code for the button's click event handler:

```
decimal TotalPrice = 0M;
foreach (Book item in MyBooks)
{
    TotalPrice += item.Price;
}
this.label1.Text = "I have " +
MyBooks.Count.ToString()
+ " books, which cost $" + TotalPrice.ToString();
```

6 Run the application to test your code.

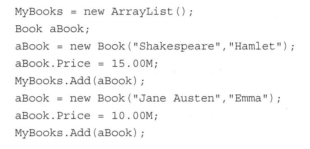

Inheritance basics

Another key feature of objects and classes is called Inheritance. This is where one class is based on another class, automatically picking up all its properties and methods. It is an excellent way to create a customized class that borrows most of its features from an existing class. It is important to understand Inheritance, even if you don't expect to make much use of it in your own code, since the .NET Framework classes frequently use it. In addition, all Visual C# classes inherit from the base **object** class.

An example

A class in C# can only directly inherit from one class. However, the parent class may itself inherit from another class, and so on, to form a chain of inheritance.

An audio book is like a printed book, with a title and author, but has additional features like a Narrator. By creating an AudioBook class, inherited from Book, you can reuse your existing code.

1　In your Book project, choose File > Add new item, selecting a class and calling it AudioBook.

2　Using one of the techniques described on page 79, add a private string field mNarrator and a Narrator property to get and set mNarrator.

3　Find the beginning of the class, and amend the class statement by adding : Book at the end. What this means is that AudioBook inherits from Book:

```
public class AudioBook: Book
    {
    //etc...
```

4　Find the constructor for AudioBook and amend it as follows:

```
public AudioBook(string author, string title,string narrator): base(author,title)
    {
    this.mNarrator = narrator;
    }
```

If you miss out the call to base, then C# will attempt to call the base constructor with no parameters. The Book class will not accept that, so in this case the code will not compile.

Note how the constructor has been modified. The declaration ends with a colon, followed by the **base** keyword. It means: call the constructor of the class from which this one inherits, passing these parameters.

Once you change the type of the Object you are adding to the ListBox, Visual C# prompts for the correct arguments.

5 Add the following override method to the AudioBook class:

```
public override string ToString()
{
return this.Title + " read by " + this.Narrator;
}
```

Now you can amend the code to list AudioBooks instead of Books. Instead of:

```
listBox1.Items.Add(new Book("Lewis Carroll","Alice in Wonderland"));
```

you write:

```
listBox1.Items.Add(new AudioBook("Lewis Carroll","Alice in Wonderland","John Baker"));
```

What this demonstrates is that although the AudioBook class does not include code for the Title and Author properties, it gets them anyway, because it inherits from the Book class.

To test the new class, adapt the Book List project on page 81 to list AudioBooks instead (or as well).

Notice how the new list shows the Narrator instead of the author, because of the new ToString() function added to the AudioBook class.

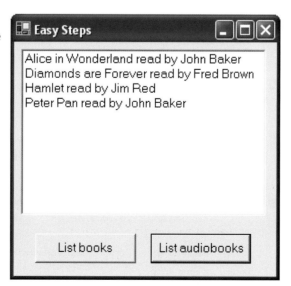

This is the book list amended to list AudioBooks instead of Books

More about inheritance

Inheritance can be chained

You can create a chain of Inherited classes. So you might create an AudioNovel, which inherits from AudioBook and adds special features relevant to Novels. However, you cannot inherit from more than one class at a time.

AudioBooks are still Books

In the rules of object orientation, an AudioBook is a Book, but a Book is not an AudioBook. This means that:

```
Book myBook;
myBook = new AudioBook("John", "Some Title","Jane");
```

This point is important because it ensures that an object always behaves in the correct way for its type. For example, you might have a Automobile object and an inherited DieselAuto object, both with FillWithFuel methods. If a DieselAuto object were assigned to an Automobile variable, you would still want FillWithFuel to invoke the DieselAuto version of the method.

is perfectly valid code. An important point: if you add:

```
MessageBox.Show(myBook.ToString());
```

then the MessageBox will display the AudioBook's version of ToString(), with the narrator instead of the author. However:

```
MessageBox.Show(myBook.Narrator);
```

will raise an error, because the Book object does not have a Narrator property. Equally:

```
AudioBook myBook = new Book("Jane","Some title");
```

will raise an error, because you cannot assign a Book object to an AudioBook variable. There is not enough information in a Book to make a valid AudioBook.

Casting

As an example, you might have a ListBox that included both Books and AudioBooks. Using code like this, you can detect whether a particular object is a Book or an AudioBook and access the full features of both object types.

If you have a Book variable that refers to an AudioBook object, you can convert it to an AudioBook. When you are not sure, the **is** operator lets you test the object's type. Here's an example:

```
Book myBook;
myBook = new AudioBook("John", "Some Title","Jane");
    if (myBook is AudioBook)
    {
    MessageBox.Show(((AudioBook)myBook).Narrator);
    }
```

Encapsulation and interfaces

Encapsulation is a feature of object orientation, and fully supported by C#. It refers to the way that the inner workings of an object are hidden from other objects. For example, the Book class stores the Author name in a private variable called mAuthor. However, no other code can read mAuthor directly, or even know that it exists. At some future date, you could rewrite mAuthor to use a different private variable, and code that uses Book objects could continue to do so without being changed. So three benefits of encapsulation are:

The classic definition of object-orientation includes four features: Encapsulation, Inheritance, Polymorphism, and Abstraction.

- It makes code more manageable by letting you break down a project into smaller parts

- It makes code more robust by preventing code from being used in unexpected ways

- It makes code more reusable, by allowing you to change implementation details without breaking compatibility

Understanding interfaces

The word "interface" is another piece of object-oriented jargon. An object's interface is the part that can be seen by other objects: mainly its properties, methods, and events. C# also has a special type called an Interface. The meaning is similar: an Interface type describes the public view of an object, but without any implementation.

If you implement an interface, you must add the necessary properties and methods that the interface requires. It is like a contract: when you implement the interface, you agree to support all its members.

You cannot create an object directly from a C# Interface. Instead, you can create a class that implements that Interface, and then create an object from that class. By convention, Interface types begin with I. It is important to know what Interfaces are since they crop up in the Visual C# documentation. For example, the IList interface is implemented by a number of familiar objects, including Array, ListBox.ObjectCollection, and ToolBar.ToolBarButtonCollection.

Although a class can only inherit from one other class, it can implement any number of interfaces.

The syntax for implementing an interface is similar to that for inheritance:

```
public class BookList: IList
```

Overloading and overriding

In the AudioBook class on page 84, the ToString() method is declared with the **override** keyword:

```
public override string ToString()
```

Not all functions can be overridden, only those originally declared with the virtual or abstract modifier. Methods declared abstract exist solely to be overridden, as they have no implementation of their own.

This keyword indicates that the method has the same name as a method in a base class, and is to be used instead of the base class version. An overriding method must take the same arguments as the method it overrides.

The alternative to overriding is **name hiding**, which uses the **new** modifier:

```
public new string ToString()
```

Overloading and overriding are features that support what object-oriented jargon calls Polymorphism: the ability for the same thing to have many forms.

The keyword new indicates that this method is unrelated to the method of the same name which is implemented by its base class. Name hiding is risky as it introduces inconsistent behavior. In this example, if an AudioBook object were assigned to a variable myBook of type Book, then myBook.ToString() would call the Book version of ToString(), not the AudioBook version. If you use **override**, the AudioBook version will always be used, which is often what you want.

Overloading

Overloading takes place when a class has several methods with the same name, but different parameters. Which version gets used depends on what arguments you supply. The Visual C# editor shows when you call an overloaded method, by popping up a scrollable number.

Overloading is a handy way to provide default values for your class. For example, say you want to give the Book class a second constructor that takes only a Title parameter. In this constructor, you could call the existing constructor passing the value "Unknown" for the Author.

The editor pops up a scrolling list of overloads.

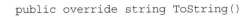

```
this.Font = new Font(
        ▲ 3 of 13 ▼  Font.Font (string familyName, float emSize, System.Drawing.FontStyle style)
        familyName:
           A string representation of the System.Drawing.FontFamily object for the new System.Drawing.Font object.
```

Static members

Most of the time programmers work with object instances, rather than calling code in a class directly. In fact, normally trying to call code in a class without first creating an object of that class raises an error. There is a way to get round this rule, and that is through static members. For example, all books have an ISBN number, part of which represents the publisher. You might want to add a method to the Book class that returns the publisher from an ISBN. This function is not a characteristic of a particular book, but a general utility. Therefore, you can make this a static member:

In object-oriented jargon, an object member refers to any field, property, function or sub belonging to the object.

```
public static string PubFromISBN (string ISBN)
    {
    string result = string.Empty;
        if (ISBN.StartsWith("07607"))
            {
            result = "Barnes & Noble";
            }
        else if (ISBN.StartsWith("0596"))
            {
            result = "O'Reilly";
            }

        //etc
    return result;
    }
```

It is common to have classes in which all the members are static. These classes are not intended to form the basis of object instances, but simply group together useful functions, types and constants. An example is the .NET Math class.

You can call a static member without creating an object instance. Because it belongs to the class, you must use the class name rather than the instance variable:

```
MessageBox.Show(Book.PubFromISBN("1840780290"));
```

Code in static members cannot access non-static members of its class. For example, there would be no sense in referring to the Title property within PubFromISBN, since Title is only set in instances of Book.

Static fields

You can also have static fields. This is like a global variable accessed through the class.

Protected and internal members

The idea of public and private variables or other class members is straightforward, but sometimes it is better to have something in between. The Book class has a private variable called mTitle, declared like this:

```
private string mTitle;
```

It is good that other classes cannot directly access mTitle, but it is possible that you might want the AudioBook class to be able to see it. Currently, even though AudioBook inherits from Book, code in the AudioBook class cannot access mTitle:

```
public override string ToString()
    {
    return this.mTitle + " read by " + this.mNarrator;
    }
```

This code will not compile. There are two ways to fix it. Either use the public property, this.Title, or else change the declaration of mTitle in the Book class:

```
protected string mTitle;
```

The **protected** specifier means that mTitle is visible to classes that inherit from Book, as well as in the Book class itself.

Internal members

The **internal** specifier restricts access in a different way. Anything declared **internal** is visible throughout the project, but not from other projects. This is only relevant once you start building libraries for use by other projects, or developing multi-project solutions.

Keep members internal if they are not intended to be accessed directly by users of a library class.

Internal protected

It is possible to inherit from classes defined outside your own project; in fact, it happens every time you create a class that inherits from a .NET Framework class, like a Form. Therefore, **internal** members may not be visible to inherited classes. If you want a member to be both **protected** and **internal**, you can use them together.

Understanding Namespaces

In the early days of programming, variables with the same name were a common source of bugs or other problems. It was especially dangerous to use a common word like Author or Title as a variable name. Programmers used to try and avoid the problem by using prefixes or postfixes, such as easysteps_author, easysteps_title.

Modern programming languages are less prone to this kind of problem. Objects help matters, because most variables are qualified by object names, as in MyBook.Author, MyBook.Title. But what if Microsoft introduced a Book class into the .NET Framework, or you installed a third-party library with a Book class?

See the next page for how to simplify Namespace use with the using directive.

Namespaces are the solution. A Namespace does nothing except to group together classes so that they have a unique identifier. Visual C# projects have a default namespace, which initially is the name of the project (with spaces replaced by underlines). If the Book class is in a project called BookExample, you can refer to it by the full name of BookExample.Book. Namespaces are created with the namespace statement, followed by curly brackets which surround the namespace:

You can use the same Namespace in more than one file, to group a number of classes together. You can also use a dot in the Namespace, as in: MyNameSpace.Bookstuff.

```
namespace MyNameSpace
    {
    public class Book
    {
    //...
    }
}
```

This would let you reference the Book class as MyNameSpace.Book. Namespaces can be nested, for further differentiation.

Edit the default project namespace from Project Properties

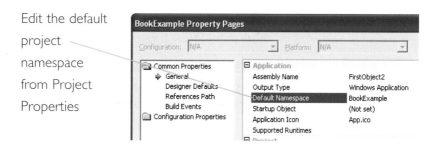

The using directive

Namespaces are a great way to prevent ambiguous class names, but can make code verbose. For example, it would be tedious to type:

```
BookExample.MyNameSpace.Bookstuff.Book myBook;
```

If you are looking for a globally unique namespace identifier, a good tip is to use your Internet domain name, if you have one, as part of the namespace.

every time you needed to refer to the Book class.

The solution is the **using** directive. This directive comes at the top of a file, before any class or namespace declaration. It means that any class or other types within the specified namespace will be found automatically, without having to give the fully qualified name. In the above example, you could put:

```
using BookExample.MyNameSpace.Bookstuff;
```

at the top of a C# file. Then you could simply type:

```
Book myBook;
```

and C# will be able to find the class.

More about using

A **using** directive must use the fully qualified namespace, right back to the root namespace. So in the above example, you could not omit BookExample. However, you could leave out some of the names to the right:

The using directive is just a way of identifying classes. That is all it does. It does not load any libraries or execute any code. It follows that its use is always optional. If you don't mind the extra typing, you can always manage without it.

```
using BookExample.MyNameSpace;
```

In this case, you could refer to the Book class like this:

```
Bookstuff.Book myBook;
```

Finding a namespace

The **using** directive does not guarantee that Visual C# can find the namespace. If the namespace is in your project, there is no problem. Otherwise, you have to add a reference to the libraries that contain the namespace. See page 112 for more details.

Another using statement

C# also has a **using** statement, that has a completely different purpose. It is important not to confuse the two. See page 94.

Object lifetime

It is possible to maintain references to objects for longer than you really intend. If this happens, your application will use more memory than it needs to, or in the worst case its memory usage may constantly increase. This is known as a memory leak. You can track down problems like this with tools called profilers.

How long does an object last? Normally, it lasts for as long as there is a valid reference to it. When there is no longer a valid reference to the object, such as a variable that represents it, then the object is in effect dead; no code can access it. For example, an object that is declared within a method will cease to exist once the method ends, or even earlier if its scope is less than the entire method, unless the code returns a reference to the object or sets a reference to the object elsewhere in the project. With the same exceptions, an object that is referenced by a class variable will cease to exist when the parent object dies.

It is important to understand that variables are not themselves objects. Rather, they refer to objects. For example, the following code uses one variable but two objects:

```
Book mybook = new Book("Shakespeare","Hamlet");
mybook = new Book("Austen","Emma");
//first book object is now dead
```

It follows that you can deliberately kill an object by removing the last reference to it:

```
mybook = new Book("Austen","Emma");
mybook = null;
//kills the object
```

Using Dispose

Always call Dispose when you have finished with an object that implements iDisposable. Otherwise, resources are not cleaned up and might cause problems later in the application.

Since the .NET Framework uses a technique called garbage collection (see page 78), you cannot know exactly when an object will be removed from memory. Most of the time that does not matter. However, some objects use resources such as files, database connections, or Windows API graphical resources. These are known as "unmanaged" resources because they are not native .NET objects. With such resources, it is important to free them specifically rather than waiting for garbage collection. C# has the Dispose method for this purpose. This special method frees all the unmanaged resources. When necessary, you can also implement Dispose (as part of the IDisposable interface) in your own classes.

The important thing is always to call Dispose when you have finished with objects that implement IDisposable. C# can do this for you via the using statement – see page 94.

The using statement

The using statement is a convenient feature that saves having to call Dispose. The using statement takes an object as an argument, and is followed by a block marked by curly brackets. At the end of the block, C# calls Dispose on the used object. For example, the following code draws a line using a Pen object. The Pen uses an unmanaged Windows resource, so it has a Dispose method.

```
private void Form1_Paint(object sender,
System.Windows.Forms.PaintEventArgs e)
{
    Pen p = new Pen(Brushes.Blue,2);
    using (p)
    {
    e.Graphics.DrawLine(p,2,2,200,200);
    }
    //Dispose is called automatically
}
```

It is good practise to take advantage of the using statement, since it makes for more reliable code.

You can also instantiate the object within the using statement:

```
using (Pen p = new Pen(Brushes.Blue,2))
```

Using only works with IDisposable
The using statement only works with objects that implement iDisposable. Otherwise the compiler will report an error.

What if you forget to Dispose?
If you forget to Dispose an object, most code will still run without problems. In most cases, the Dispose method is called in the object's destructor, so that when the garbage collector frees the object, Dispose will be called anyway.

However, in some cases forgetting Dispose could cause your code to fail unpredictably, or to use more memory and resources than it should. In general, if there is a Dispose method then the author of the class intended it to be called.

When not to Dispose
You should only dispose objects you create. System objects, such as Brushes.Blue in the above example, should not be Disposed in your code.

Visual Studio Tools

Visual Studio's tools and wizards are powerful but can be confusing at first. This chapter describes essential features like the menu editor, the debugger and the reference manager. It also explains how to set Visual Studio options so you can work the way you want.

Covers

Creating a menu

Most Windows applications use a menu to give users full control. It is easy to add a menu bar to a Visual C# project.

1 Start a new project and add a MainMenu control to the form. Next, select the form itself, and check that in the Properties window the Menu property is set to mainMenu1. Click in the menu space at top left, where the words Type Here may appear. Type File.

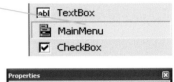

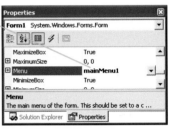

If you put an "&" character before a letter in a menu caption, it will make a shortcut key. When the menu is displayed, the shortcut letter will be underlined.

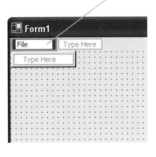

To make a separator line, type a hyphen character as the Text property.

2 Continue to work on the menu so that it reads File, Edit and Help along the top, and below File, add an entry for Open.

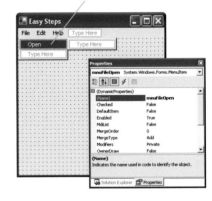

3 Select each menu item in turn, and set its name in the Properties editor. Use a consistent naming system, such as mnuFile, mnuFileOpen, etc.

It is particularly important to name menu items carefully, because with a lot of items called MenuItem1, MenuItem2 and so on it is hard to know which is which.

4 Run the project and notice how the menu you created is fully active, although the options don't yet do anything.

Customizing a menu

There are several ways in which Visual C# menus can be customized. This is done through properties.

The Enabled and Visible options control how the menu item behaves. If Enabled is not checked, the menu will be grayed out and will not trigger any action. If Visible is not checked, the menu will not appear at all

There is a difference between a shortcut key selected from the drop-down list, and creating a shortcut key with the "&" character. The first kind is more powerful, since it immediately carries out the menu action. The second kind only operates when actually navigating a menu. The menu first has to be activated with Alt.

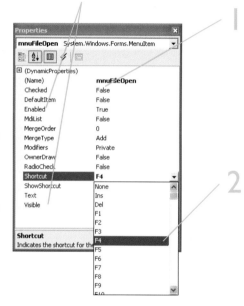

Choose the Checked option to create a menu which has a tick mark to show an option is selected.

Choose a shortcut key to have the menu action performed whenever the key combination is pressed.

If you set a Shortcut key, set the ShowShortcut property to True to have the shortcut appear automatically as part of the menu text.

This menu features a submenu and a shortcut key combination

This is a checked menu

Creating a pop-up menu

Windows applications often use a pop-up menu, which usually appears as a result of clicking the right mouse button. The menu which appears usually varies according to what object the mouse is over when the right button is pressed. Follow these steps:

When should you use a pop-up menu? The name Context Menu is a good clue. They are ideal for situations where the user may see an on-screen object and wonder what options they have. It is easier to right-click an object, than to hunt through a range of menu options at the top of the window.

Place a ContextMenu control on a form. It appears as an icon below the form, and when it is selected, the Context Menu appears in the menu bar area of the form. Click on the ContextMenu and type in some menu entries.

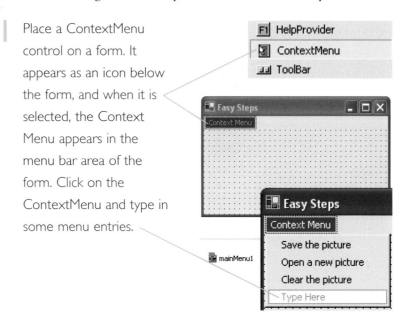

Place a picture box on the form. Set its ContextMenu property to the name of the ContextMenu.

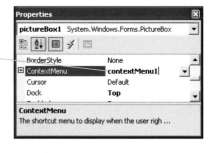

This example also has the Image property of the PictureBox set to an image, and the SizeMode set to StretchImage, but the example works without needing to set these properties.

Run the application and click the right mouse over the picture. The menu you defined opens as a pop-up menu.

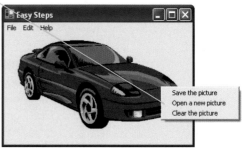

Making a menu work

The menus you have created look nice, but they do not actually do anything yet. This page explains how to write code that runs when the menu option is chosen.

The method that runs when an event occurs is called an event "handler". That helps to distinguish between the event, and the code that responds or "handles" the event.

Select the Context menu icon below the form, so that the ContextMenu is visible in the form's menu bar. Select each menu item and set the name property to something suitable, such as mnuSavePicture,

mnuOpenPicture etc. Then select a menu option and double-click. The code editor opens at the Click event handler for that menu option

To write code that actually saves the picture, use the Save method of the Image class.

If you find this technique awkward, you can also create an event handler using the properties window. First select the menu item for which you want to create an event handler. Then click the Events icon on the properties window toolbar, and double-click the event in the list in order to create the handler. If the event handler already exists, you can use this technique to jump to that point in the code.

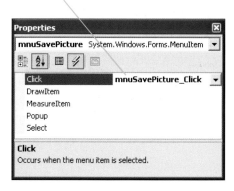

Changing menus at runtime

The best Windows applications protect the user from options that are irrelevant or impossible. For example, a word-processor should not have a Save option when no document is open. The most common technique is to disable or hide menu options according to the current state of the application.

This example uses the application described in "Creating a pop-up menu" on page 98. When you right-click a picture, a pop-up menu appears which includes Save and Clear options. If there is no picture present, the Save and Clear options should be disabled.

The secret is to write code that changes the Enabled property of a menu between True and False. For example, here is how you can write code for the Context Menu's Popup event to enable or disable the Save and Clear options:

This code will only run if your menu items have the names shown. You can change the names of menu items in the Properties window.

Create this code by selecting the ContextMenu on the form, clicking the events icon in the properties window, and double-clicking the Popup event. Then type the code into the Popup event handler.

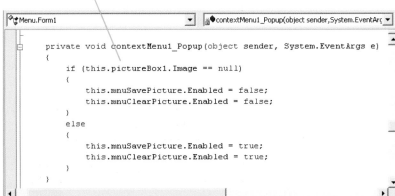

```
private void contextMenu1_Popup(object sender, System.EventArgs e)
{
    if (this.pictureBox1.Image == null)
    {
        this.mnuSavePicture.Enabled = false;
        this.mnuClearPicture.Enabled = false;
    }
    else
    {
        this.mnuSavePicture.Enabled = true;
        this.mnuClearPicture.Enabled = true;
    }
}
```

You can also hide menu items completely by setting the visible property to False.

When you run the application and right-click the picture, the pop-up menu will show disabled Save and Clear options if there is no picture loaded. Otherwise, the options will be enabled.

Another useful property is Checked. By changing this from False to True, you can have a tick appear beside a menu. This lets users see at a glance whether a particular option is selected or not, without having to open a dialog box.

Working with the code editor

As you work with Visual C#, much of your time is spent writing and editing code in the code editor. Although it looks simple, this editor has many features which make your work easier.

The features of the editor can be customized from the Tools > Options dialog.

Syntax checking

When you build or run a project, Visual C# detects syntax errors such as typing errors or impossible expressions. The problem expression gets a wavy underline. Hover the mouse over the text, and an explanation shows in a ToolTip.

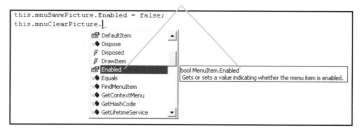

```
if (this.pictureBox1.Image == null)
{
    this.mnuSavePicture.Disabled = true;
    this.mn System.Windows.Forms.MenuItem' does not contain a definition for 'Disabled'
}
```

When you work in the editor, the work area can get too small because of other windows. Press Shift+Alt+Enter to hide the other windows and work full-screen. Press it again to bring them back.

AutoList members

As you type a dot, a list of properties and methods pop up. Select the right one and press Tab or Space to complete it. As you select each option, a ToolTip of further information also appears.

```
this.mnuSavePicture.Enabled = false;
this.mnuClearPicture.
```

- DefaultItem
- Dispose
- Disposed
- DrawItem
- Enabled
- Equals
- FindMenuItem
- GetContextMenu
- GetHashCode
- GetLifetimeService

bool MenuItem.Enabled
Gets or sets a value indicating whether the menu item is enabled.

Quick Info

Hover the mouse over any variable or class name in your code, and a ToolTip pops up with information about its declaration and type.

```
if (this.pictureBox1.Image == null)
{
    this.mnuSavePicture.E System.Drawing.Image PictureBox.Image
                          Gets or sets the image that the System.Windows.Forms.PictureBox displays.
```

If you don't have the code for the variable or method, because it is in a library, then Go To Definition takes you to the object browser instead.

Go To Definition

Right-click any variable or method name and a pop-up menu appears. One of the most useful options is Go To Definition, which jumps to the place where that variable or method is declared.

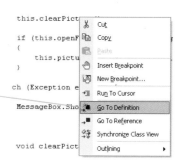

```
this.clearPict
if (this.openF
{
    this.pictu
}
ch (Exception e
MessageBox.Sho
void clearPict
```

- Cut
- Copy
- Paste
- Insert Breakpoint
- New Breakpoint...
- Run To Cursor
- Go To Definition
- Go To Reference
- Synchronize Class View
- Outlining

Outlining and auto-insertion

Outlining

The Visual C# code editor lets you expand and collapse sections of code for easier navigation.

In Visual C# there are two outlining modes. By default, Automatic Outlining is selected. Every method can be expanded or collapsed by clicking on the small + or - symbol.

If you right-click and choose Outlining > Stop Outlining, then Visual C# is in manual outlining mode. You can select a block of text and choose Hide Selection, again from the Outlining menu, to collapse and later expand the selection of your choice. Outline sections can be nested.

Auto-reformatting

Visual C# can automatically reformat your code. This can make is easier to follow, by lining up matching curly brackets and providing intelligent indents. You can reformat an entire document by selecting it all first (Edit > Select all).

Code before and after formatting

Dynamic Help

If you display the Dynamic Help window (an option on the Help menu), then Visual Studio automatically displays likely Help entries depending on what you are typing or what is selected.

Using the Clipboard Ring

When you are working in the code editor, you will often want to cut, copy and paste code. The standard Clipboard only holds one piece of code at a time, which can be annoying. The Clipboard Ring lets you keep more than one section of code on a clipboard.

The Clipboard Ring is a section of the Toolbox. When you start working in the code editor it is empty.

The Clipboard Ring works independently from the Windows clipboard. You could copy and paste from another application without disturbing its contents.

Select some code and choose Copy. The text is added to the Clipboard Ring.

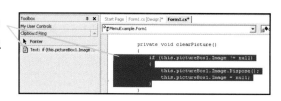

As you continue to work, the Clipboard Ring fills with further snippets of code.

To use the snippets, drag from the Clipboard Ring into the code editor.

If you prefer to work entirely from the keyboard, use Ctrl-Shift-V to paste from the Clipboard Ring. By default it pastes the last code copied, but if you press it repeatedly it cycles through all the snippets so you can find the one you want.

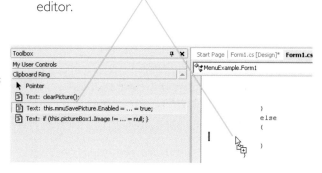

Using Find

Finding your way around a small project is easy, but gets harder as projects become larger, perhaps involving several projects combined into a solution. Visual Studio's Find tools are a quick and efficient way to track down what you are looking for. There are essentially three Find tools, two of which also have a Replace option.

The Find tools can be accessed from the Edit > Find and Replace menu.

Replace is a valuable tool, but can easily break your code, especially if you Replace All without prompts. Replace in Files is especially dangerous. Perform a Find first, to check out the matches and make sure that they are really what you want to change.

The basic Find or Replace dialog searches for strings and goes to the first occurrence. Even when the Find window is closed, the F3 shortcut in the code editor will go to the next occurrence.

If you want to change the name of a class or class member, just change it where it is first defined. The compiler will pick up the calls that become invalid, and you can fix them one by one. This is safer than Replace All.

Find (or Replace) in Files is the most powerful search. This finds the matching string in any file within the specified scope. Results appear in a Find window, and double-clicking a Iresult line opens it in the editor.

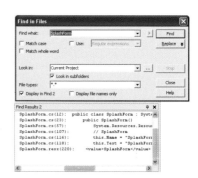

Use Find Symbol to search for an object, variable, or other C# symbol. Results appear in the Find Symbol Results window.

Introducing the debugger

Many programs do not work as you expect the first time you run them. The reason is that computers are unforgiving of typing errors, and just one letter wrong in 1000 lines of code is enough to stop your program working. Other problems are programs that work, but too slowly; or programs that work most of the time, but occasionally produce wrong results.

Normally, the program code is invisible when it is running, but the key feature of the debugger is that it lets you watch your program run line-by-line. You can also pause the program to inspect the current value of variables.

What if your program is in an infinite loop? Press Ctrl+Break to stop it running and open the debugger.

Basic debugging

1 To watch your program run line-by-line, start it running by choosing Step Into from the Debug menu.

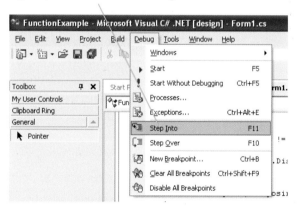

See page 107 for an explanation of other debugging options, including Step Out and Step Over.

2 As soon as the program hits some C# code, the code window opens with a small arrow showing which line is active. Press F11 to step into the next line of code or Shift-F5 to stop debugging.

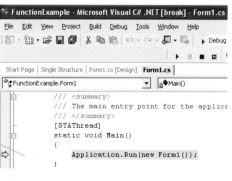

More about debugging

When the debugger is active there are several ways to get information about your program:

1   Rest the mouse pointer over a variable to see its current value:

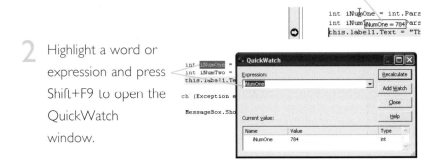

2   Highlight a word or expression and press Shift+F9 to open the QuickWatch window.

The Command/Immediate window lets you try out commands and test or change the value of variables while your program runs. The Command window has two modes. In Command mode, it offers a command-line interface for Visual Studio. For debugging, Immediate mode is more useful. To enter Immediate mode, choose Immediate from the Debug > Windows menu, or from the Debug toolbar.

Changing the value of a variable during debugging is one way to test "what-if" scenarios, or to fix one problem temporarily in order to continue testing another aspect of your code.

1   Type "?" followed by a variable or expression to see its value. Use "=" to assign a new value to a variable.

2   Use the Debug toolbar to select the Immediate window, or a range of other options.

Using breakpoints

When a program is of any significant size, stepping through all the code takes too long, especially when most of it is working fine.

Visual C# lets you set breakpoints, so that the program runs as normal until it hits the line you have marked. At that moment, the program pauses and the debugger opens.

How to set a breakpoint

You can also set and remove breakpoints by pressing F9.

To set a breakpoint, open the code editor. Click with the mouse in the left margin. A dot appears, showing that a breakpoint is set. When you run the code it will pause there. To remove the breakpoint, click on the dot.

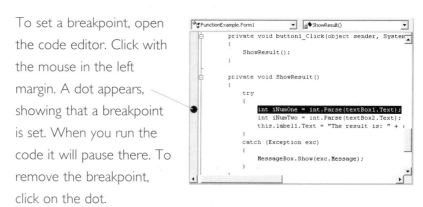

Using Step Over

A feature called Step Out is similar to Step Over. Step Out runs the remaining code in the current procedure without stepping, and resumes stepping at the next opportunity. To use Step Out press Shift+F11 or choose it from the Debug menu.

If you are stepping through a procedure which calls into a method for which you also have the code, such as another method in your class, then Visual C# will follow the code from the procedure, into the function (Step Into), and out again. This nesting can become deep as one method calls another. If you want to concentrate on the code in the current method, you can use Step Over or press F10 to move through the code. Then, Visual C# runs the code in the called method without stepping through it.

This code is about to call a user-defined method. Press F11 to step through the function, or F10 to run it without stepping through line-by-line.

```
private void button1_Click(object sender, System
{
    ShowResult();
}

private void ShowResult()
{
    try
    {
        int iNumOne = int.Parse(textBox1.Text);
        int iNumTwo = int.Parse(textBox2.Text);
```

The Locals and Watches windows

When you are debugging, it is essential to keep track of the value of variables. Visual Studio makes this easy with three tool windows:

You can add a variable to the Watches window by drag-and-drop. Select the word in the editor, and drag it to the Watches window. This only works while debugging.

- The Locals window lists all the variables which are local to the current procedure or function in a list, with their values

- The Watches window lets you choose which of your program's variables you want to keep an eye on, and displays them with their values, updated automatically as the program runs

- The Autos window is an automatic version of the Locals window. It shows all the local variables in the current statement and in the three statements on either side of the current statement. The idea is to guess what variables you are most likely to be interested in

All these windows can be selected via Debug > Windows.

When objects are listed in these windows, they appear with + signs. You can drill down into the object's members and their values by clicking the + sign.

The Autos window   The Locals window

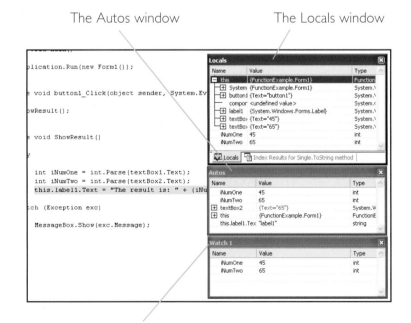

The Watches window

Tracking down errors

Some programs compile and run fine, but fail with an error when certain actions are performed. When that happens, Visual C# pops up an error dialog. There are several options.

If you or another user is running the application outside the development environment, and an error like this occurs, a different dialog appears. The exception is reported, and the user can choose to continue or quit. It is preferable to avoid this kind of dialog by trapping errors — see page 118 for details.

It is often worth noting the exception and looking it up in online Help if necessary

When available, Ignore means ignore the error and try to continue

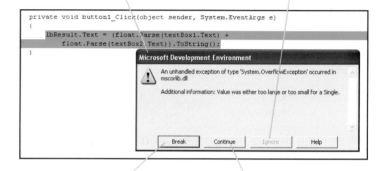

```
private void button1_Click(object sender, System.EventArgs e)
{
    lbResult.Text = (float.Parse(textBox1.Text) +
        float.Parse(textBox2.Text)).ToString();
}
```

Microsoft Development Environment

An unhandled exception of type 'System.OverflowException' occurred in mscorlib.dll

Additional information: Value was either too large or too small for a Single.

[Break] [Continue] [Ignore] [Help]

Click Break to go into debug mode on the current line

In principle, Continue means carry on and let any error-handling code catch the error. This usually has the effect of terminating the application.

You can control how the debugger handles exceptions in the Debug > Exceptions dialog. If you set it to break into the debugger whenever exceptions are thrown, then you will see this dialog even if the exception is handled. In that case, Continue will allow the application to continue running.

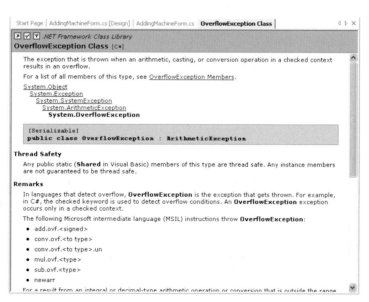

Start Page | AddingMachineForm.cs [Design] | AddingMachineForm.cs | **OverflowException Class**

.NET Framework Class Library
OverflowException Class [C#]

The exception that is thrown when an arithmetic, casting, or conversion operation in a checked context results in an overflow.

For a list of all members of this type, see OverflowException Members.

System.Object
  System.Exception
    System.SystemException
      System.ArithmeticException
        System.OverflowException

[Serializable]
public class OverflowException : ArithmeticException

Thread Safety

Any public static (**Shared** in Visual Basic) members of this type are thread safe. Any instance members are not guaranteed to be thread safe.

Remarks

In languages that detect overflow, **OverflowException** is the exception that gets thrown. For example, in C#, the checked keyword is used to detect overflow conditions. An **OverflowException** exception occurs only in a checked context.

The following Microsoft intermediate language (MSIL) instructions throw **OverflowException**:

- add.ovf.<signed>
- conv.ovf.<to type>
- conv.ovf.<to type>.un
- mul.ovf.<type>
- sub.ovf.<type>
- newarr

For a result from an integral or decimal-type arithmetic operation or conversion that is outside the range

This particular error is caused by assigning a value to a single which is greater than 3.402823e38. The problem can be solved by catching the error and reporting the reason to the user.

Customizing the Toolbox

One of the best features of Visual Studio is that you can add new components to your project. You can add two kinds of components. Components written in the .NET Framework are one kind, while the other is an ActiveX control.

What is a .NET control?

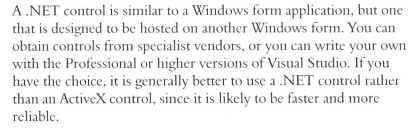

A .NET control is similar to a Windows form application, but one that is designed to be hosted on another Windows form. You can obtain controls from specialist vendors, or you can write your own with the Professional or higher versions of Visual Studio. If you have the choice, it is generally better to use a .NET control rather than an ActiveX control, since it is likely to be faster and more reliable.

What is an ActiveX control?

An ActiveX control is a Windows executable designed to be hosted within another application. It uses a technology called COM, which is a long-established Windows standard. ActiveX controls are also used on Web pages.

Adding controls to the Toolbox

To use a .NET or ActiveX control, you first have to install it on the Visual Studio Toolbox. Here is how to do it:

You will probably find ActiveX controls on your system which you cannot use in Visual Studio. Some ActiveX controls are installed for runtime use only. To use them in Visual Studio you have to buy a licence. Others are not designed to work with Visual Studio. Sometimes a faulty Windows installation prevents controls from working properly.

If you have the choice, .NET components are preferable to ActiveX controls, since they do not require COM Interop (see p.112 for more information about COM Interop).

1. Right-click the Toolbox and choose Customize Toolbox.

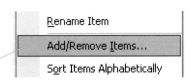

2. ActiveX controls are listed under COM components. Native .NET controls are listed under .NET Framework components. Check the components required and click OK.

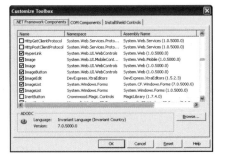

The term component includes visual and non-visual classes. The term control means a visual component you can host on a form and set properties from the properties window.

3. The selected controls appear in the Toolbox at the foot of the appropriate section. You can use them in the normal way.

Using the Add-in Manager

Another way of extending Visual Studio's powers is by the use of add-ins. Unlike ActiveX controls, add-ins are not used at runtime. Instead, they enhance the Visual Studio development environment, either adding new features or making existing features easier to use.

Using the Add-in Manager

The list of available Add-ins depends on which version of Visual C# you have installed. You can also purchase Add-ins as separate products.

1 Choose Add-in Manager from the Add-in menu. A list of add-ins appears. Click on the one you want to install.

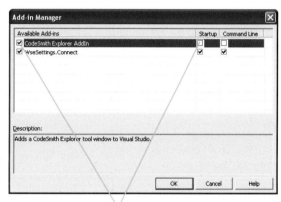

2 Check to install it for this session. Check "Startup" to have it always loaded. "Command Line" determines whether the add-in loads for command-line builds.

3 How to use the add-in depends on what has been installed. Some add-ins create menu options, while others extend functionality in other areas. The CodeSmith add-in illustrated above installs its own tool window, which can float or dock in the same way as other Visual Studio tool windows. It then enables you to generate C# code for common tasks such as creating custom collection classes. CodeSmith is not supplied with Visual C#, but is available as a third-party add-in.

You can find CodeSmith at the following web address:

http://www.ericjsmith.net/codesmith/

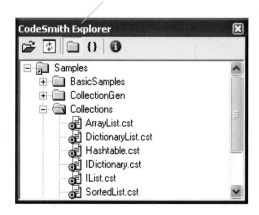

Explaining the Reference Manager

A Visual C# program is not limited to using objects that are defined by classes in the project itself. It can also use objects in other libraries or applications. To do this, you need to set a reference to the target library or application. Once the reference is set, the additional set of objects becomes available in the same way as built-in objects like buttons and TextBoxes.

If you are trying to access a documented .NET class in your code, but the compiler cannot find it, the chances are you need to add a reference. For example, it is no use adding a using directive for a class that is not included in a referenced library.

You can set a reference to other .NET objects, such as standard libraries or code in other .NET projects. You can also set a reference to Windows applications or libraries that support COM, Microsoft's older component technology. This is called COM Interop.

A COM example is when a C# program automatically fills in values in an Excel spreadsheet. From C#, you can get full control over Excel. When the reference is set, Visual C# loads a description of Excel's objects found in Excel. This enables Visual C# to check the code that controls Excel objects. These object descriptions are called "type libraries". You can also use the Reference Manager to run code compiled as COM components, such as those created by Visual C++ or Visual Basic 6.0 or earlier.

As with Add-ins and ActiveX controls, the list of available references depends on what else is installed on your system.

To open the Reference Manger, open the Solution Explorer (View > Solution Explorer), right-click the References item, and choose Add Reference....

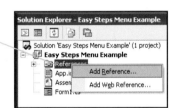

The Reference Manager is used to add or remove references to type libraries. To use it, highlight the required components and click Select. Then click OK

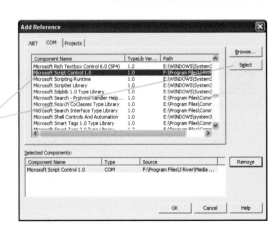

Setting Visual C# options

The Options dialog is found in the Tools menu. Using Options, you can change the behavior of Visual C# to your liking. For example, the Editor tab controls the extra features of the code editor like Auto list members.

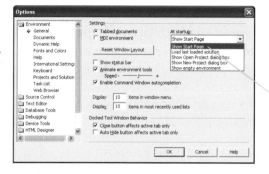

Use the Options dialog to customize Visual C# to suit the way you work

This option changes what is presented when Visual Studio starts up

Tabbed and MDI mode

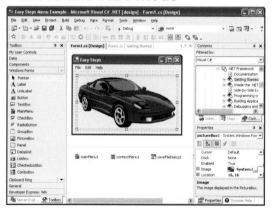

One handy option is Save Changes to open documents, in the Environment > Projects and Solutions section. Set it to Save when a program builds and runs, so that you will not lose your work in the event of a power failure or software crash.

One important option is in the Environment > General section. In Tabbed documents mode, windows form a central tabbed section

Unless you strongly prefer MDI mode, use the tabbed mode, which is the default. Most programmers find it easier to work with.

In MDI (Multiple Document Interface) mode, documents float in the centre area and can be maximized, tiled or cascaded from the Window menu

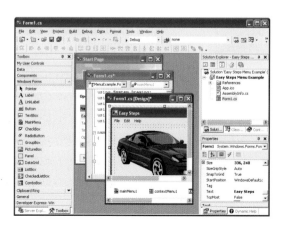

Setting project properties

The Tools > Options dialog changes the behavior of Visual Studio, irrespective of which project you are working on. There are other important options which only affect the current project. These are set from the Project Properties dialog. An easy way to find this is from the Solution Explorer.

The Standard edition of Visual C# does not include the Library option for projects.

Using project properties

The project properties are important for the correct operation of your application. Some of the options are the output type (Windows, Console or Library), the compiler options like whether debugging information is generated, the application icon, and for Web applications the target browser type (Internet Explorer 5.0, Netscape Navigator and Internet Explorer 3.0, or Netscape Navigator 4.0). You also control optimization settings and advanced features such as conditional compilation constants.

When you specify browser targets, the application should work with the specified versions or higher.

Solutions also have a Properties dialog. Its main use is to manage solutions that have multiple projects.

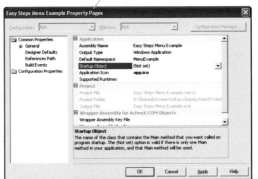

To display Project Properties, right-click the Project name (not the Solution name) in the Solution Explorer. From the pop-up menu, choose Properties. This opens the Project Properties dialog

This is where you set the Startup object, a key option in any C# application. The Startup object must be a class with a static Main method. By default it is the first form in the project, but in larger applications it is often changed to a custom class.

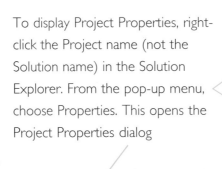

Creating a standalone application

As you learn Visual C#, you will soon create applications which you want to use without having to run them from within the programming environment. You will also want to make them available to others.

This page explains how to create a standalone executable. To distribute programs to others, you need to learn about Setup projects, explained on pages 140–144.

Visual C# applications are not truly standalone. They use the Common Language Runtime, which is part of the .NET Framework. The Common Language Runtime must always be available.

1   To create a standalone executable, load your project and choose Release from the Configuration drop-down list. Then choose Build Solution from the Build menu. Make sure it builds without errors.

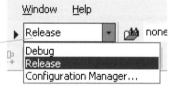

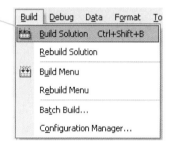

The default icon for an application is a dull rectangle, but you can choose another icon from Project Properties, in the General section. This example is one of the ones supplied with Visual C#.

2   Next, find your application in the Release subfolder of the bin folder (in the folder where your project files are stored). If you are not sure where Visual C# put them, select the project name in the Solution Explorer and press F4. The Project Folder is listed in the Properties window.

If you use the application regularly, but are also still working on the code, it is best to make a copy for your regular work. During coding the latest version may not always be usable.

3   You can run the executable by double-clicking the icon. You can drag it to the Start menu to make it easy to find. You can move it to another location on your machine, provided you move any dependent files with it, if there are any.

Where Help files come from

Most professional software comes with Help files. Press F1 in a dialog box, and custom help appears for that dialog.

This page does not tell you everything about creating Help files, but gives you an idea of what is involved.

Microsoft HTML Help workshop is for creating HTML Help files. These consist of HTML pages compiled into a single Help file with a .CHM extension. The Help file includes topics and indexing.

Third-party Help software is easier to use and more productive than that supplied by Microsoft. Some software allows for creating both online Help and a printed manual.

The first step is to build a .CHM Help file for your application. The next step is to set links to the Help file. The easy way to do this is by adding a HelpProvider component to a form. This appears below the form.

The HelpProvider control in the Toolbox

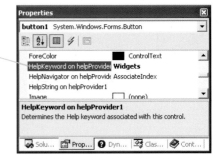

When you add a HelpProvider to a form, you can set its HelpNameSpace to a Help file of your choice. After adding a HelpProvider, other controls on the form get three new properties: HelpKeyword, HelpNavigator and HelpString. Set the HelpNavigator to a type of search in the Help file, such as a topic entry or keyword index. Set the HelpKeyword to the word to search for. If there is no HelpNameSpace set, use the HelpString to create a pop-up F1 help for the control. These are somewhat like a ToolTip, but only appear when the user presses F1.

If you have Web access, visit Microsoft's website for the information about new Help authoring tools.

Setting help properties for a Button control. This only activates when the Button has the focus and the user presses F1.

C# Techniques

This chapter explains important techniques for creating powerful C# applications, including dealing with errors, printing, graphics, and creating setup routines.

Covers

Chapter Six

Catching errors with exceptions

Applications written with .NET are safer for the user than many alternative programming systems. A .NET application is unlikely to cause your system to crash, for example. However, there are still plenty of reasons why errors occur. Most are caused by errors in your code, or by failing to anticipate all the ways in which your program may be used. Here is a simple example:

Users may not know what to make of dialogs like this one. Wherever possible, it is better to anticipate errors and deal with them in code.

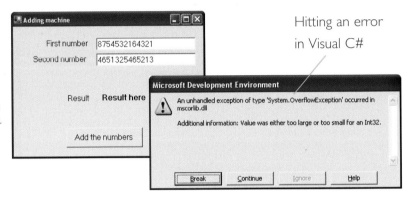

Hitting an error in Visual C#

You can see the reason for the error if you see the code:

```
lbResult.Text = (int.Parse(textBox1.Text) +
        int.Parse(textBox2.Text)).ToString();
```

The int.Parse method converts a string into an integer. This works fine with small numbers, but if the result is above 2,147,483,647 the application stops with an overflow error. Even if you used an Int64, it is possible to enter a number large enough to cause an overflow. The user might also mistakenly enter a word such as "one" in the text box, causing an "input string not in the correct format" exception.

Exceptions

Errors like these are called Exceptions, because they are regarded as exceptional circumstances. There are two main techniques for preventing them:

- Validation, to stop the exceptional circumstance occurring

- Exception handling, to deal cleanly with exceptions that occur

Here is how to improve the last example by adding an exception handler:

The term "exception handler" means a section of code which only runs when an exception has occurred. Its purpose is to recover gracefully from the problem.

This line begins the protected block

This line starts a block of code that only runs when an exception has occurred

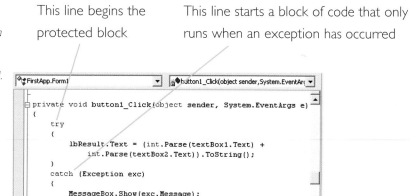

```
private void button1_Click(object sender, System.EventArgs e)
{
    try
    {
        lbResult.Text = (int.Parse(textBox1.Text) +
            int.Parse(textBox2.Text)).ToString();
    }
    catch (Exception exc)
    {
        MessageBox.Show(exc.Message);
    }
}
```

By checking the message property of the Exception object, an appropriate message is displayed

Trying out the Exception handler

Here is what happens when you run the new code:

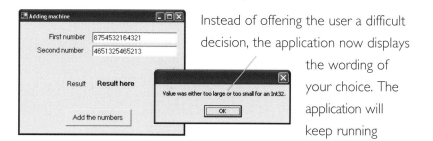

Instead of offering the user a difficult decision, the application now displays the wording of your choice. The application will keep running

See the next page for a better exception handler.

Even this is not an excellent exception handler. It might not tell the user in plain English why the error has occurred. Because it is a universal exception handler, the programmer cannot really know what message to display, and has to resort to the Message property of the Exception object. Therefore, the best code looks for likely exceptions and deals with them individually.

A better exception handler

The .NET Framework has numerous Exception classes which inherit from the base Exception class. There are two ways you can exploit this. You can inspect the Exception in a generic exception handler with code like:

```
if (exc is ArithmeticException)
```

Alternatively, you can have multiple **catch** statements:

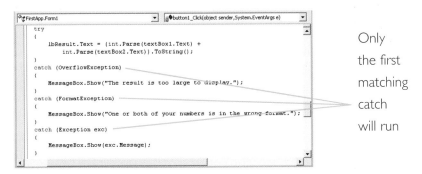

Only the first matching catch will run

This message could be further improved by adding code, for example to check which number was too large. Good error messages are clear, avoid technical language, and explain what the user needs to do next. It can also be helpful to include a telephone number for technical support.

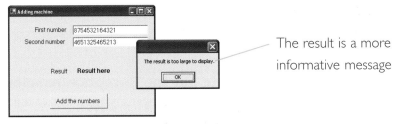

The result is a more informative message

If you have multiple **catch** statements, they must be ordered from the most specific to the least specific, as once a matching **catch** statement is found, no others will run. You can check the hierarchy in online Help. For example, OverFlowException inherits from ArithmeticException. Therefore, you could look first for an OverFlowException, next for an ArithmeticException, and last for a generic Exception.

Don't use exception handlers as a primary means of validation. That makes for slow code. Instead, use validation, but include exception handlers for unpredictable or truly exceptional cases.

You can also use **catch** on its own, without including an Exception type. This will catch any error, but it's more convenient to include a reference to the Exception object.

Wrapping code in an exception handler does not slow down performance much, but if triggered, exception handlers are slow. Generally, it's better to prevent errors with validation, and to use exceptions as a last resort.

Try... Finally

A great feature of C# is that the **try** code block can also include a **finally** clause. Code following the **finally** statement always runs, whether or not there was an exception. **Finally** can be combined with **catch**, as a **try... catch... finally** block, or you can use it on its own as **try... finally**.

Here is an example:

The Finally block can save a lot of conditional code. Use it for code that must always be executed, for example to clean up resources.

When you use finally, make sure the try block starts in the right place. For example, you only want to close a file if it was successfully opened.

```
StreamReader sr;

//Read a log file
try // try to open the file
{
    sr = File.OpenText(@"c:\MyData\MyLog.txt");
    try // try to read the file
    {
        string s = sr.ReadLine();
        while (s != "")
        {
            // do something with s
        }
    }
    finally //Always close the file
    {
        sr.Close();
    }
}
catch (Exception exc)
{
    MessageBox.Show(exc.Message);
}
```

File handling is prone to errors. The file might not exist, or it might be opened exclusively by another application, or it may contain unexpected characters. In the above example, the first **try** block is focused on opening the file. If the code gets as far as the second **try** statement, then the file is open and a **finally** clause is used to ensure that it is closed. It is no good using a single **try** block, since if the file was not opened, attempting to close it then will itself raise an exception. A nested block like this deals with both the possibilities.

Exceptions bubble up

When an exception occurs, it will bubble up through the code until it finds a valid exception handler. If one is not found, the user gets the default .NET exception handler. That means you do not have to have exception handlers in every block of code. Think about what will happen if an exception occurs, and make sure it is caught somewhere helpful.

Using validation

Validation is about making sure input is correct before attempting an operation. Although exception handling is a great way out of trouble, it is better to detect and prevent the problem before it reaches an exception handler.

The ErrorProvider

Add an ErrorProvider control to a form in order to report errors to the user. The ErrorProvider has a SetError method, which takes a control and a string. If you pass it a string containing a message, then a little red icon appears by the specified control. When the user hovers the mouse over the control the message appears. If you pass an empty string, the icon and message go away. You can use the ErrorProvider to inform the user of validation problems.

The ErrorProvider control

Creating a validation function

Validation is a common requirement, and you will be likely to need a few utility functions to test for common problems. The following function tests whether a string is valid as a number:

```
ExceptionExample.Form1          isValidNumber(string s)

    private bool isValidNumber(string s)
    {
        char [] chararray = s.ToCharArray();
        bool hasDecimalPoint = false;
        for (int i = 0; i < chararray.Length; i++)
        {
            char ch = chararray[i];
            if (ch == 46) //46 is a decimal point
            {
                if (hasDecimalPoint) return false;
                else
                {
                    hasDecimalPoint = true;
                    continue;
                }
            }
            if ((ch > 57) || (ch < 48)) //tests for a numeric char
            {
                return false;
            }
        }
        return true;
    }
```

To handle the Validating event, first find the control in the left-hand dropdown list, and then select the Validating event from the right-hand dropdown list.

If you set the Cancel property of the CancelEventArgs to True, the user cannot submit the value, but remains focussed on the control until the problem is corrected. You can set the ErrorProvider without setting the Cancel property, in which case the red icon appears without trapping the user in the control.

It is possible to obtain controls called Masked Edit controls. These have built-in validation and formatting, making it quicker to create validated forms.

The Validating event

Now that we have a function that will test for a number, it can be put to use. Many Visual C# controls have a Validating event that you can use to check data input. Here is an example:

```
private void textBox1_Validating(object sender,
    System.ComponentModel.CancelEventArgs e)
{

    if (! isValidNumber(textBox1.Text) )
    {
        this.errorProvider1.SetError(textBox1,"You must type a number");
        e.Cancel = true;
    }
    else
    {
        this.errorProvider1.SetError(textBox1,string.Empty);
    }
}
```

Validation can take many different forms. It does not have to be done in a Validating event. Sometimes validating code needs to look up values in a database or refer to the value of other fields on a form. It is always important to think about the user's experience. That means giving a simple, clear and polite explanation of what is wrong and making it easy to fix. For example, a message that simply reported "Invalid number" would be irritating not helpful.

Some programmers prefer to validate a number of controls together, say when an OK button is clicked, rather than individually.

Trapping the user

The above example leaves the user trapped on the TextBox until a valid number is entered. It is important to offer an escape route, for example by writing an event handler for the KeyDown event of the TextBox:

```
if (e.KeyCode == Keys.Escape)
{
this.errorProvider1.SetError(textBox1,string.Empty);
textBox1.Text = string.Empty;
}
```

Now the user can press ESC to clear the error.

Helping the user

One of the best ways to avoid errors is by making it hard for the user to make mistakes.

1. Use the Enabled and Visible properties

Most applications have buttons and menu options which are not always relevant. Worse, if used at the wrong moment they might cause an error. For example, you might have a Close option which closes a document. If there is no document open, Close means nothing.

Set the Visible property for options that are completely irrelevant to the current state of the application. Set the Enabled property to give the user a clue that, if something else happens, that option will become available. For example, Edit > Cut is a good candidate for enabling and disabling rather than hiding completely.

The solution is to either hide or disable irrelevant or dangerous options. In your Open code, you could have a line like this:

```
mnuFileClose.Enabled = true;
```

When the last document is closed, you can have:

```
mnuFileClose.Enabled = false;
```

If you prefer to remove the option completely, use the Visible property.

Disabled menu options

The same options with the Enabled property set to True, after a document has been opened

2. Use ToolTips, progress bars and status bars

Instant Help text that appears when an option is selected, or when the mouse is over a control, is a very useful to the user. See the next page for how to show ToolTips.

To change the shape of the mouse-pointer, set the Cursor property for a form or a control. See online Help for the possible values, which include Cusrsors.Waitcursor and Cursors.Arrow.

If an operation takes a significant amount of time, set the mouse pointer to an hourglass and show progress in a status bar or progress bar whenever possible. Users need to see something happening, in case they assume the application has crashed.

How to use ToolTips

The ToolTip control has its own properties, which determine whether ToolTips are active, how long it takes for them to pop-up, and how long they stay visible once shown.

1 Drag the ToolTip control to a form. It appears as an icon in the area below the form.

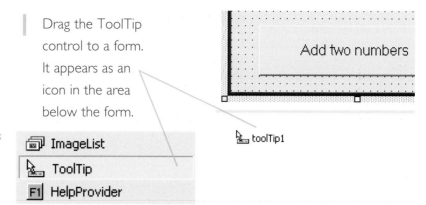

2 Select a control on the form, such as a button, and set the "ToolTip on ToolTip1" property to a help text of your choice.

3 Run the project, and hover the mouse over the button to see the ToolTip.

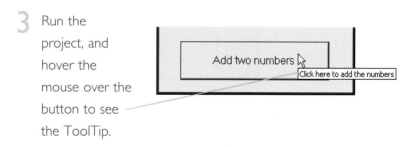

You can also set ToolTip properties in code. The advantage would be that you could vary the ToolTip according to the state of the application. For example, a disabled button could have a ToolTip giving the reason why the button is disabled. When enabled, it could explain what the button does. If you set a ToolTip in code and also in the Properties window, the code will override the property setting.

Normally you will just have one ToolTop control on a form, which works for all the other controls. It represents a convenient way to make settings that affect all the ToolTips on a form.

Printing with Visual C#

A frequent requirement is to print information from Visual C#. For example, you might want to print customer details from a form. Unfortunately printing is somewhat complex. There is no single Print method, so you have to write code that outputs text or graphics piece by piece to the printer. However, it is not difficult to get started with printing, as this example shows.

Other print controls include PrintDialog, which lets users select a printer and choose page numbers, a PageSetupDialog control for setting margins and page layout, and a PrintPreviewControl that lets you show previews without using the PrintPreviewDialog.

Start a new project and lay out a form with labels, textboxes and a button as shown. Add a PrintDocument and a PrintPreviewDialog control.

Since printing is complex, some third-party components for Visual Studio include built-in printing features, so that you can more easily create printed reports.

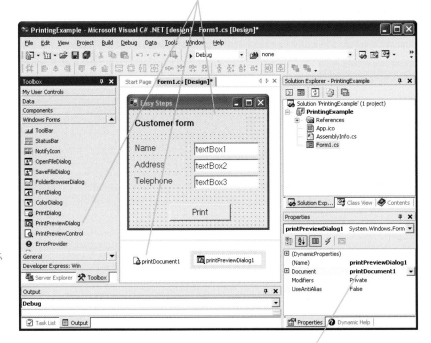

Set the PrintPreviewDialog's Document property to PrintDocument1.

Add one line of code to the button's Click event:

```
this.printPreviewDialog1.ShowDialog();
```

...cont'd

4 Select the PrintDocument1 icon and then click the events icon in the properties window. Double-click PrintPage to create a PrintPage event handler.

This code places the lines of text a fixed distance apart, determined by the lineheight variable. For more accurate positioning, you can use the Font.GetHeight method to discover the height of the characters, and add a little extra.

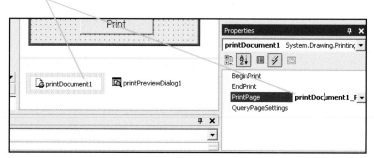

5 Add the following code to the PrintPage event:

```csharp
float xpos, ypos;
float lineheight = 50;
using (Font f = new Font("Arial", 24,
FontStyle.Bold))
    {
    xpos = e.MarginBounds.Left;
    ypos = e.MarginBounds.Top;
    e.Graphics.DrawString("Customer form", f,
Brushes.Black, xpos, ypos);
    }
using (Font f = new Font("Arial", 12,
FontStyle.Regular))
    {
    ypos += lineheight;
    e.Graphics.DrawString("Name: " + textBox1.Text,
f, Brushes.Black, xpos, ypos);
    ypos += lineheight;
    e.Graphics.DrawString("Address: " +
textBox2.Text, f, Brushes.Black, xpos, ypos);
    ypos += lineheight;
    }
```

This code makes use of the += operator. This is shorthand for expressions like:
ypos = ypos + lineheight.

If you are not sure which fonts will be available, use Arial, Courier or Times New Roman. These come with Windows and are almost always installed. Note the use of the using statement with the fonts, to ensure resources are freed.

6 Run the application to test it. When you click Print, a page preview appears. Click its Print icon to send it to the printer.

More about printing

The key to printing in Visual C# is the PrintDocument. This component lets you set up the page through its DefaultPageSettings property, and specify printer settings through its PrinterSettings property. You can also set the DocumentName, which shows up in the Windows printer queue so that users can check the status of their printout. The PrintDocument has a Print method, and it is this that kicks off the printing process.

Not all applications require print features. Feel free to skip this topic or to come back to it at a later date.

The PrintDocument knows how to print, but it does not know what to print. This is what the programmer has to supply in code. When the Print method is called, the PrintDocument fires a PrintPage event, passing an argument of the type PrintPageEventArgs that includes information about the page settings as well as a Graphics object. The Graphics object represents the surface of the paper, and has methods like DrawString, DrawLine and DrawImage that let you output text and pictures to the page. The code has to specify exactly where each line of text or image is placed. In order to calculate these positions, there are methods that measure the length of a string of text. Naturally you have to specify the font to use before these will work correctly.

Printing multiple pages

A long document will span multiple pages. To make this work, the programmer sets the HasMorePages property of the PrintPageEventArgs argument, within the PrintPage event handler. It is False by default, meaning that only one page is printed. If it is set to True, then PrintPage gets called again, and so on until all the pages are printed.

PrintPreview

Although printing is complex, Visual C# makes it very easy to offer PrintPreview. This is good for the user, as you can check how the page is turning out without wasting lots of paper.

Tips for readable code

When you are enthusiastic about a project, it is easy to bang out lines and lines of code. Later on, when you come to correct or improve the code, it is important to be able to find your way around easily. Here are some tips:

1. Use auto-format

At any time in the code editor, Ctrl-A followed by Ctrl-K and then Ctrl-F will auto-format your code.

Edit > Advanced > Format Selection does a good job of formatting your code. It uses plenty of white space along with sensible indentation to make it easy to see the program structure. You might be able to do a better job manually, if you have strong preferences, but for most people letting Visual C# do the formatting is the best option.

2. Comment generously

Like white space, comments are ignored at runtime so they do not slow down your code.

Ideally, comment each method and property to show what they are there for. If you are working in a team, show when they were written, and who by, and when last amended. If there are parameters, say what they are for.

Visual C# makes it easy to insert comment blocks before each method. Click the insertion point before the method, then type ///. It will be expanded to an outline summary block.

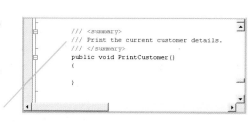

```
/// <summary>
/// Print the current customer details.
/// </summary>
public void PrintCustomer()
{

}
```

Any line that begins with two forward slashes is a comment. You can also add comments to the end of a line, following two forward slashes.

When you use the special comment blocks inserted with ///, Visual C# creates an XML **summary** tag within the comment. This is used by Visual Studio's intellisense to provide tooltip help about the class member when you use it in your code. You can also generate XML documentation when you build, by setting this option in Project Properties.

If you add some code to work around a problem, add a comment to explain why that code was added. Otherwise, you or someone else may come along later, not know why it is there, and delete it.

Following code standards

The names you choose for functions, procedures and variables make no difference at runtime. They do, however, make a difference to the readability of your code. Professional programmers have been known to deliberately obscure their code, simply by changing all the names to meaningless ones. More often, though, programmers want to make code easy to understand.

1. Use descriptive names

It is better to have names that are descriptive rather than short. Better to have a function called:

```
GetIncomeFromEmployeeId(int EmployeeID)
```

than this concise alternative:

```
GetInc(int ID)
```

2. Use a naming convention

Visual C# is case-sensitive, and you can make good use of upper and lower case in the names you choose.

Programmers love to argue about what is the best way to choose names. Schemes for devising names are called naming conventions. For example, it can be useful to identify the type of an object or variable by using a consistent prefix, for example using iSomething for an integer. Another common convention is to begin private class members with a lower case letter, and public members with an upper case letter.

You can find FxCop on the official .NET resource web site:

http://www.gotdotnet.com

The design guidelines are part of the Visual C# online help.

Microsoft provides a full set of design guidelines for the .NET Framework, covering naming conventions and other matters. There is also a utility called FxCop that will help you to follow them.

In this book, the examples often use the default Visual C# names for controls, like button1 and label1. This is to help putting together short, quick examples; it is not good practise in real programming work. You will have lots of forms with controls called button1 and label1, and tracing through the code will not be easy.

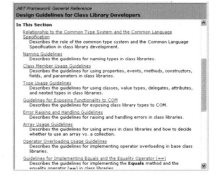

Managing multiple forms

Most of the examples in this book have only used one form. To build a complete application, you will often find that you need more than one form. Here is how you include additional forms in your project:

1 In a new or existing project, from the File menu, choose Add New Item.

2 Choose a Windows Form, accepting the default name of Form2.cs.

Should you close a form with Hide or Close? Although both close a form, they do different things. Hide leaves the form in memory, so it is good if you need to refer to the values of its controls, or will be displaying it again soon. Close removes the form from memory and is good if you want to conserve system resources.

3 The new form is a class. To use it in your code, first declare an object of that class, and then call its Show() method. If you want to use the form as a modal dialog, which must be closed before the user continues with anything else, call ShowDialog() instead.

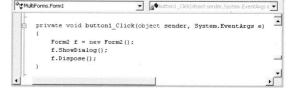

If you use a form as a dialog, make sure the form stays in memory until you have finished reading values from the form's controls. To help you do this, the Close method does not immediately destroy a form shown modally with ShowDialog.

4 You can close the form at runtime either by allowing the user to click the Close button at top-right, or in code with the Close() method. If you want the form to persist after it is closed, close it with Hide() and keep the object variable in scope so you can show it again.

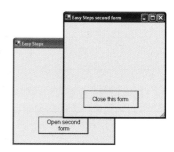

Introducing MDI

Applications which use multiple forms can get untidy, especially if the forms are displayed non-modally. If there are several applications open, it can even be hard to tell which form belongs to which application.

MDI stands for Multiple Document Interface. It is a way of managing multiple windows by trapping them within a master window. In Visual C#, this master window is called a MDI form. Then, forms can be displayed as MDI children, which can be moved within the master form, but not outside it. Most word-processors and spreadsheet applications use MDI.

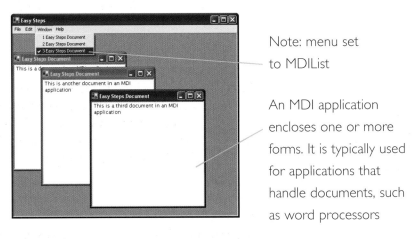

Note: menu set to MDIList

An MDI application encloses one or more forms. It is typically used for applications that handle documents, such as word processors

MDI forms have a property called ActiveMdiChild, which gives you a reference to the child form that currently has the focus. This enables you to target code to the correct form.

Working with MDI forms

There is not enough space here for a full description of MDI. Getting started is easy, though. First, begin a new application. Then set the main form's IsMdiContainer property to True. Finally, when you create a child form, set its MdiParent property to the MDI container form. For example, if you were opening the child form from a button or menu on the main form, you could write:

```
Form2 f = new Form2();
f.MdiParent = this;
f.Show();
```

MDI forms have some special features. A menu can be set to MDIList, which means it shows a list of open windows and activates the one selected. This is important, especially if a document is maximized, as some documents may be out of view.

Starting a C# application

You have to create Sub Main yourself. First, add a module to the project. Then, add a procedure to the module called Sub Main. Typically, it will include a command to show a form.

All Visual C# projects have a startup object. This determines which code runs first. The startup object is set in Project Properties, and can be any class with a static Main method. By default, Visual C# generates Main for the first form in the project.

Click here to set the startup object.

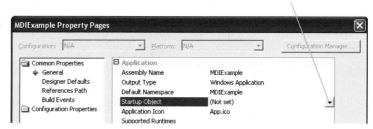

Why use a separate startup class?

Application.Run starts an application message loop. If passed a form as an argument, the application will continue to run until the form closes.

In an application which is more than trivial, using a separate startup class has several advantages. It is a convenient place to set variables to default values, open a database, or check that all the files needed by the application exist. Then you can display the initial form, using Application.Run, for example:

```
Application.Run(new Form1());
```

Including a splash screen

Starting with Sub Main makes it easy to display a splash screen. This is a form which shows while your application starts up. If the full application takes a while to load, the splash screen reassures the user that all is well. Simply include a line like:

```
SplashForm sf = new SplashForm();
sf.Show();
// show the splash
Application.DoEvents();
//allow form to paint
```

at the beginning of Main. When you have done all the initialization, continue with:

```
sf.Close();
Application.Run(new Form1());
```

How to read and write to a file

Most real-world applications need to read and write disk files. In many cases this is done for you behind the scenes. For example, if you use Visual C#'s database features, then the disk access is handled by the database engine. You do not need to worry about opening or closing disk files directly.

Even so, knowing how to read and write information on a disk is a valuable skill. For example, you might want to write and display a log file. This sample shows how you can write out a text file and then load it into a window:

1. Start a new project. On the project's main form, add a TextBox with its Multiline property set to True and Scrollbars set to Vertical, and a button.

2. Double-click the button to open its Click event handler. Before writing any code, scroll up in the editor and add:

```
using System.IO;
```

If you develop this project further, a good plan would be to give writeFile a parameter so that you could pass it a line of text to write.

at the top. Then create two void methods, writeFile and readFile. Then add the code shown to the Click event handler.

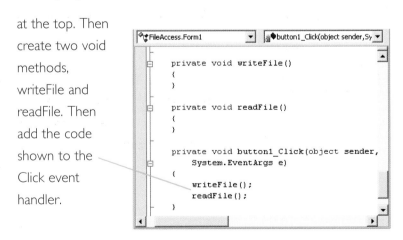

3 Now add the code for the two methods. Here it is:

This example does not teach you all you need to know about reading and writing files. It does, however, show how easy it is to get started.

```csharp
private void writeFile() {
    StreamWriter sw;
    try {
        sw = new StreamWriter(File.Open(@"C:\EasyLog.txt",
            FileMode.OpenOrCreate));
        try {
            sw.BaseStream.Seek(0, SeekOrigin.End);
            sw.WriteLine("Log entry added at: "
                + DateTime.Now.ToShortTimeString());
            sw.Flush();
        }
        finally {
            sw.Close();
        }
    }
    catch (Exception exc) {
        textBox1.Text = "Error: " + exc.Message;
    }
}

private void readFile() {
    StreamReader sr;
    try {
        sr = new StreamReader(File.Open
            ( @"C:\EasyLog.txt", FileMode.Open));
        try {
            textBox1.Text = sr.ReadToEnd();
        }
        finally {
            sr.Close();
        }
    }
    catch(Exception Exc) {
        textBox1.Text = Exc.Message;
    }
}
```

This is how the code works. StreamWriter and StreamReader are objects that know how to write and read text files (not binary files). The File object's Open method returns a FileStream object, which is used to create the StreamWriter and StreamReader objects. The StreamWriter seeks to the end of the file and writes a line, then Flush is called to make sure it is actually written to disk, and finally it is closed.

The StreamReader has a convenient ReadToEnd method that reads the entire contents of a file into a String, which becomes the Text property of the TextBox.

4 Run the project and click the button several times to add entries to the log.

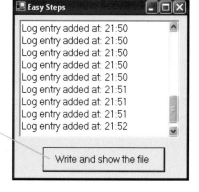

Drawing graphics

Users rightly expect Windows applications to display information graphically. Using Visual C#'s graphic methods, you can draw your own charts and graphs on forms and picture boxes.

How to draw in a PictureBox

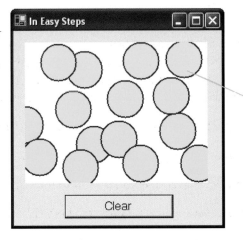

This example uses a form, a PictureBox and a button. Each time the mouse clicks on the PictureBox, a filled circle is drawn where the mouse lands.

2 Place the following code in the PictureBox's MouseDown event handler:

```
//create a bitmap to persist the drawing
if (pictureBox1.Image == null) {
Bitmap bm = new Bitmap(pictureBox1.ClientSize.Width,
pictureBox1.ClientSize.Height);
pictureBox1.Image = bm;
}
//get a graphics object
Graphics g = Graphics.FromImage(pictureBox1.Image);
Pen pn = new System.Drawing.Pen(Color.Red,2);
//draw on the graphics
g.DrawEllipse(pn,e.X - 25,e.Y -25,50,50);
g.FillEllipse(Brushes.Yellow,new RectangleF(e.X-
24,e.Y-24,48,48));
//clean up
pn.Dispose();
g.Dispose();
//repaint the pictureBox
pictureBox1.Refresh();
```

In this example, the reason for using the event MouseDown rather than Click is that MouseDown gives you the current position of the mouse relative to the object.

3 The code for clearing the PictureBox is short:

```
if (this.pictureBox1.Image != null) {
pictureBox1.Image.Dispose();
pictureBox1.Image = null;
}
```

How this code works

The .NET Framework does not have any simple graphical controls like lines or shapes. Instead, you draw on a control surface using graphical methods. The code shown uses several objects:

Graphics: Provides methods for drawing to a surface.

Bitmap: An object representing a bitmap image.

Pen: An object that controls how lines are drawn.

Brush: An object that controls how fills are drawn.

It is possible to draw on a PictureBox without creating a bitmap, but such drawings will by default disappear whenever the control has to be repainted, for example if it is covered by another window and then uncovered. The Bitmap object persists the image. Therefore, the code creates a bitmap in memory and draws on that. The PictureBox does not automatically repaint itself when the bitmap changes, so the code calls its Refresh() method to force a repaint.

Objects like Graphics, Bitmap, Pen and Brush use system resources. These objects have a Dispose method that you should call once you have finished with them, to free these resources, except in the case of system objects like members of the Brushes class.

The Graphics classes are based on a Windows API (Application Programming Interface) called GDI+. This is a powerful API with many options for textured, transparent, blended and gradated drawing that can produce some highly sophisticated effects. You can also use text in creative ways.

Creating a shared event handler

Sometimes you will find that several buttons or other controls need to run identical code. Using Visual C#, you can have one event handler respond to the events from more than one control. The following example shows how you might use this technique to have a search button for each letter of the alphabet (although only the first four letters are implemented here, and rather than actually search a database it just displays a messsage):

1 Place a Button on a form, size it small, and choose Edit > Copy. Then choose Edit > Paste. Place three similar copies on a form, and finally a TextBox.

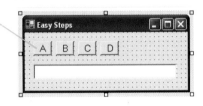

2 Name the buttons BtnA, BtnB, BtnC and BtnD. Give them Text properties of A, B, C and D in turn.

3 Now double-click BtnA to open its Click event handler. Add the following code:

```
Button btn = (Button)sender;
textBox1.Text = "Searching for names beginning: " +
btn.Text;
```

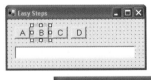
In this code, notice how the sender object is assigned to a Button variable, in order to read off the Text property of each Button. For this to work, you must ensure that the code only handles Button events. Another idea is to check the type of the sender variable before doing the cast.

4 Select btnB in the form designer. In the properties window, click the Events icon. Click on the drop down arrow by the Click event and select BtnA_Click. Do the same for btnC and btnD. Run the code to test it.

Interrupt with DoEvents

You can usually interrupt an errant program by pressing Ctrl+Alt+Del and terminating it from the Task Manager. It is not a sign of good software, though.

Nothing is worse than accidentally triggering an option that takes a long time, and then not being able to cancel it. For example, imagine you have a procedure that does lengthy processing in a loop, such as a routine which calculates how many prime numbers there are up to one million. That takes a significant amount of time. The problem is that while C# is racing round the loop, the rest of the application is dead. You cannot have a Cancel button, because no Click event will fire until the loop is done. Worse still, if a bug causes an infinite loop, the user will not be able to break in.

Using DoEvents

There are several ways around this problem. The simplest is to use DoEvents. This command hands control back to Windows, so that Click events or other actions can be processed before the loop continues. Here is how to do it:

Add two buttons and a label to a form. Declare a class-level variable:

```
private bool cancelFlag;
```

For the button which starts the long process, add this code:

If you use DoEvents, there is a possibility that the user may click again on the button which triggers the loop. You should prevent this either by disabling the button (as here) or by setting a flag so that the loop will not run again.

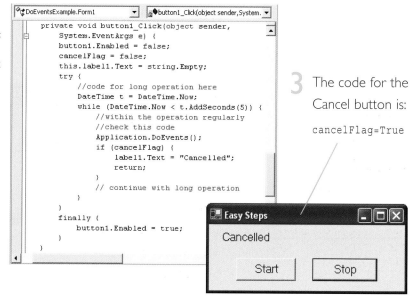

```
private void button1_Click(object sender,
    System.EventArgs e) {
    button1.Enabled = false;
    cancelFlag = false;
    this.label1.Text = string.Empty;
    try {
        //code for long operation here
        DateTime t = DateTime.Now;
        while (DateTime.Now < t.AddSeconds(5)) {
            //within the operation regularly
            //check this code
            Application.DoEvents();
            if (cancelFlag) {
                label1.Text = "Cancelled";
                return;
            }
            // continue with long operation
        }
    }
    finally {
        button1.Enabled = true;
    }
}
```

The code for the Cancel button is:

```
cancelFlag=True
```

Using a Setup Project

If you find the Package and Deployment Wizard hard to work with, investigate third-party alternatives such as InstallShield or WISE.

When you have completed a Visual C# application, you will naturally want to distribute it to others. Unfortunately, installing a Windows application is not always straightforward. The main reason is that most applications are dependent on the presence of a number of files, code libraries, and often a database engine. These may be present on your development machine, but not on everyone else's PC. In addition, many files cannot just be copied, but need to be registered in some way. For Visual C#, it is essential that the .NET Framework runtime files are installed, in the same version as used by your application. Finally, there is the business of adding Start menu or Desktop shortcuts, so that users can find the application.

All this means that you cannot generally just copy an application onto someone else's hard disk and expect it to work. Instead, you need to create a set of installation files which include a Setup application, and copy them to CD or make them available for download on the Web. This application does the work of checking versions, copying files, registering any ActiveX controls and finally installing program shortcuts onto the Start menu. Fortunately, Visual Studio has a wizard which will create this Setup application for you. The following example demonstrates how this works with a simple application, the Calculator created on page 57.

Getting started

It is important to add the Setup project to your project, rather than starting a new solution, since it makes it easier to configure. If you use the Setup wizard, available in some versions of Visual C#, the same applies.

Having checked that your application is fault-free, compile and save it with the configuration set to Release. Leaving the solution open, choose File > Add Project > New Project.

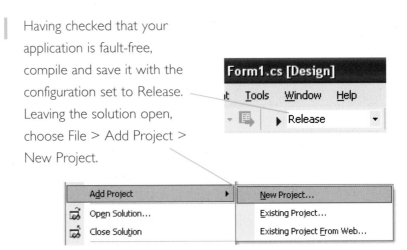

2 In the New Project dialog, choose Setup Project and call it Easy Steps Calculator Setup.

3 Click the Application Folder in the File System view. Then right-click in the blank area to the right, and choose Add > Project Output.

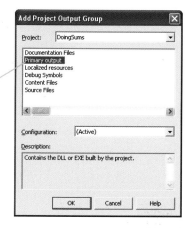

It is essential to have the right folder highlighted in the left panel, and to right-click in the right panel in order to get the correct menu.

If your screen does not look like this, right-click the Setup project in Solution Explorer and choose View > File System.

4 In the Project Output dialog, choose Primary Output and click OK. If you have other files such as Help files or bitmaps, right-click again and choose Add File.

If you ignore a Detected Dependency, you must be sure that the requisite files are already installed on the target machine. It is only worth doing if you want to keep the install size down to a minimum. For a downloaded Setup, you could offer a choice between a full or partial install, for those who already have the right version of the .NET Framework installed.

5 In the Solution Explorer, notice how the .NET runtime is listed under Detected Dependencies. This is a warning that your project may not run unless other files are added. Other projects may have other dependencies listed.

...cont'd

Some dependencies can be resolved by adding a merge module. To see a list of merge modules, right-click the setup project and choose Add and then Merge Module. The exact list will vary depending on what is installed on your machine. A merge module is a packaged setup routine that can be inserted into another setup routine.

The currently active folder is distinguished by a slightly different icon, showing an open folder. The "User's Program Menu" refers to the Programs section of the Start Menu. If you want to access other special folders, such as the top level of the Start Menu, right-click the File System panel and choose Add Special Folder.

The Setup also creates an uninstall program. You can see this after running the Setup, in the Add/Remove Programs part of Control Panel.

6 If you know that your users will already have the .NET Framework runtime installed, you can ignore the dependency. Otherwise, you can include the .NET runtime setup with your own setup routine. The .NET setup is called Dotnetfx.exe. Users can also obtain this from Microsoft's web site, or from the Windows update site at http://www.windowsupdate.com. The Visual Studio .NET Setup Project can't itself install the runtime, although this can be done using other setup tools. Simply have your users run Dotnetfx.exe before running your setup.

7 Now return to the File System view. In the left-hand panel, select User's Programs Menu. In the right-hand panel, right-click and choose Create New Shortcut.

8 In the Select Item in Project dialog, double-click the Application Folder and then select the Primary Output. Click OK.

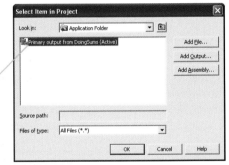

9 Rename the Shortcut to Easy Steps Calculator.

This is the name that will appear on the Start menu, as the user is unlikely to understand the term Primary Output.

10 From the Build menu, Build the setup project, or right-click the Project name in Solution Explorer and choose Build.

11 The compiled Setup.exe is in the Release folder in the setup project directory. Distribute all the files in this directory to your users.

More about the Setup Project

The step-by-step guide explained the minimum steps needed to create a setup routine for an application. However, you may want to further enhance the project. For example, the wording on the dialogs could be improved. Here is some more information about the Setup project:

The Windows Installer

The Setup Project generates files that are run by the Windows Installer service. This is a sophisticated and complex feature of Windows. The reason for the complexity of the Setup Project is the complexity of the Windows Installer itself.

Setup Project Views

The Setup Project has several views. These are as follows:

- **File System:** This is where the actual files to be installed are determined. This view is like a virtual Windows Explorer, where you add files in the location where they are to be placed on the target machine. It is important to use the Special folders, since you cannot know in advance how the target machine is configured. Special folders read the location of items like the Start menu, or My Documents folder, when the setup runs

- **Registry:** This view looks like Regedit but with an empty registry. You can add registry entries, and they will be replicated on the user's machine

- **File Type:** This is important for applications that use documents. Normally, you would create a new File Type for your document. You can associate commands with the File Type, so that when the user double-clicks a document, it opens in your application

Making an application open a document on double-click can be complex, particularly if your application might already be running.

- **User Interface:** This is the series of dialogs seen by the user. The Administrative Install is used to install setup files to a network location, from which other users can install it. When you are getting started with the installer, concentrate on the main Install sequence

- **Custom actions:** These are external scripts or executables that you can run as part of the install process. This can be a life-saver if you cannot get the Installer's built-in functions to do exactly what you require

- **Launch conditions:** You may want installation to fail in some circumstances, for example if the user has too little RAM for your application to run properly. Another aspect is whether the user might already have a later version of the application. Adding a check for this prevents trouble

Customizing the Setup Project

Most Setup features are accessed by right-click menus and by setting properties in the Properties Window. Have the Properties Window open, and click an item in one of the views to see the available properties.

Here is how to modify the dialog wording in the example Setup:

To understand how the Setup Project works, it is worth reading the section on the Windows Installer in online Help.

You can also add new dialogs. Right-click the Install sequence and choose Add Dialog. Simple options include a Readme dialog and a user license display.

Each setup project has three codes which are essential to its functioning, especially if you want to install upgrades. These are the ProductCode, the UpgradeCode and the version. When you prepare an upgrade, you must increment the version and let Visual Studio generate a new product code, but leave the upgrade code as-is.

In the Solution Explorer, select the Setup Project Name and press F4. The Deployment Project Properties are displayed. Amend the ProductName and Title, for example to remove the word Setup. These variables are used throughout the project

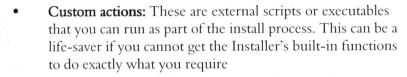

Display the User Interface view and select the Welcome dialog. In the Properties Window, modify the WelcomeText. You can use variables like [ProductName] in square brackets. Build and test the customized project

Creating Database Programs

Visual C# is ideal for managing data. It comes with a built-in database engine as well as drivers for numerous database servers. Data stored by Visual C# can also be used by other applications like Microsoft Access or Word. This chapter explains how to get started, creating an example database application for a small club. It also shows how to manage database connections, enabling you to add queries and create reports.

Covers

Chapter Seven

Introducing databases

A database is simply a collection of information, or data. In a sense, even a list in a word-processor document or spreadsheet is a simple database. Such lists are inflexible and hard to manage once they get beyond a certain size. Visual C# is able to handle small and large databases easily. You can create forms for searching, updating or reporting on data. You can also use C# code to perform calculations or process large numbers of records in one batch.

There are a few words that database programmers use in a special way. It is worth remembering what they mean.

A table

A table is a list of information organized into fields or columns. Usually each field has a fixed length.

The best way to learn how databases work is to create one. That is what you will be doing, step by step, in this chapter.

A table displayed in Microsoft Access

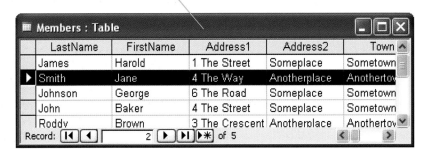

Records or rows

A record is a single row in the list. Tables are sometimes viewed a single record at a time, rather than as a list in a grid.

A database

A database is a collection of tables which are related in some way. For example, you might have a table of customers and another table of orders. Some databases only consist of one table.

Structured Query Language (SQL)

If you spend much time working with databases, you will have come across references to SQL. This is a language used to query and update data. Although you do not need to learn this to get started, it is essential for progressing beyond the very simplest of database applications.

Creating a database with Access

Access is part of Microsoft Office Professional; it does not come with Visual Studio.

Visual Studio is a great tool for building database applications, but it is a programming tool. This chapter shows how to create a database application, and to do this you will either need to work with an existing database, or create a new one. The next few pages describe how to create a database using Microsoft Access. If you want to learn database programming but do not have Microsoft Access, there are several options:

- Obtain a sample database in .mdb format, such as Northwind.mdb (or NWind.mdb) which comes with a number of Microsoft applications

- Use a different database manager, such as SQL Server, Visual FoxPro, dBase or Lotus Approach. Any database for which an ODBC driver exists should be usable from Visual C#. ODBC stands for Open Database Connectivity, and is a long-established standard for database connections in Windows

Even if you do not use Access, you will be able to duplicate the structure of the example database. You will be creating a database to manage a sports club. You can easily adapt it to store general addresses, a book or music collection, or any other kind of data.

If you already have a database you want to work with, turn to page 151.

Run Access and choose to create a new, blank database. In the File Selection dialog, navigate to C:\MYDATA, creating the folder if necessary, and type the name SPORTS.MDB.

2 When the database opens, choose the option to create a table in Design view. The Table Designer opens. Now turn to the next page to continue designing your database.

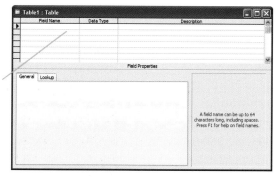

Designing a table

Now it is time to define the structure of the table. This important step determines what kind of information can be stored.

To add a field to the table, first type the name of the field in the top row of the grid. Next, check that Data Type is correct according to the table below. Finally, edit the Field Size and Required fields in the grid in the lower part of the Table Designer.

Add fields as specified in the table below. Leave any properties not specified at the default values:

The names of field types vary from one database to another. In SQL Server you would use VarChar or NVarChar (the Unicode version) for text fields, and Identity for AutoNumber. Memo types vary as well. Look for a field type that allows a large or unlimited amount of text.

NAME	TYPE	SIZE	REQUIRED
LastName	Text	30	Yes
FirstName	Text	30	No
Address1	Text	50	No
Address2	Text	50	No
Town	Text	50	No
State	Text	50	No
Zip	Text	15	No
Telephone	Text	30	No
Notes	Memo	n/a	No
ID	AutoNumber	n/a	Yes

3 Next, select the LastName row and set the indexed property to Yes > Duplicates OK. Then select the ID row and click the Key icon, to make this the primary key.

Field Name	Data Type
Town	Text
State	Text
Zip	Text
Telephone	Text
Notes	Memo
ID	AutoNumber

Table1 : Table

The Primary Key is a field or combination of fields that is guaranteed to be unique for each row. Using an AutoNumber field is a good way to be sure that no two rows have the same ID.

FIELD	PRIMARY KEY	UNIQUE
ID	Yes	Yes
LastName	No	No

The indexes required

4 Finally, click Close to save the table design. When prompted to name the Table, call it Members.

5 When you finish, the Members table appears in the Access database window. Double-click the table to open it. It will look like this, but without any names in the rows.

Members : Table

	LastName	FirstName	Address1	Address2	Town	State
▶	James	Harold	1 The Street	Someplace	Sometown	Florida
	Smith	Jane	4 The Way	Anotherplace	Anothertown	New York
	Johnson	George	6 The Road	Someplace	Sometown	Washington
	John	Baker	4 The Street	Someplace	Sometown	Florida
	Roddy	Brown	3 The Crescent	Anotherplace	Anothertown	New York

Record: 1 of 5

This page is the last time Access is used directly in this book. The rest of the work is done entirely with Visual Studio.

6 To complete the table, add some names. Add at least 3 or 4, and preferably more than that, so that you can see real data in your C# application. Click in the blank row at the foot of the table to type in a new name.

More about database tables

Using Microsoft Access introduces some key features of database tables.

Field type

Fields in a database table have a data type, similar to those used by C# for variables. You need to choose field types appropriate for the data to be stored. Some of the most important are:

Text – for strings of characters like names, addresses and telephone numbers. You can set the maximum number of characters up to 255.

These data types apply to tables in MDB format, the format used by Microsoft Access. You can also use other kinds of data tables with Visual Studio, such as FoxPro or SQL Server. These have different data types, although similar ones are available.

Integer and Long – for whole numbers. The Integer type is smaller, and can only hold numbers from -32768 to +32,767. The AutoNumber field is a Long Integer. Each record will automatically be assigned the next available number, up to 2,147,483,647.

Memo – for strings of up to 65,535 characters. You cannot specify the length. It automatically increases as needed, up to the limit.

Boolean – for True or False values.

Single and Double – for floating-point numbers. The Double can hold larger numbers and with greater precision.

Currency – for money values.

Date/Time – for date and time values.

Other field properties

Two of the fields, LastName and ID, were set as Required. That means all records in the table must have some entry for that field.

Primary Key

The ID field was indexed as Primary and Unique. It is also marked as AutoNumber. This combination means that every record can be reliably identified by its ID field. This is an essential feature of well-designed data tables.

The Data Form Wizard

The easiest way to display data on a Visual C# form is to use the Data Form wizard. Note: if the Data Form Wizard is not in your version of Visual C#, skip this section and turn to page 159. You do not have to use the Wizard.

1 Start a new Visual C# project. When the project opens, choose File > Add New Item and select the Data Form Wizard. Use the default name of DataForm1.cs, and click Open.

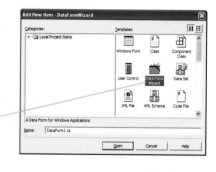

2 Click Next past the opening screen. Then the Wizard asks you to choose a dataset. Select "Create a new dataset named" and type in dsSportsClub. Then click Next.

3 The Wizard then asks you to choose a Connection. Click New Connection. The Data Link Properties dialog opens.

Depending on which data providers are installed on your system, this list may look different. The important thing is to choose the most recent JET provider. JET is the code name for the Access database engine.

4 In the Data Link Properties dialog, click the Provider tab. Then click on the line called Microsoft Jet 4.0 OLE DB Provider, and click OK.

Visual C#'s Data Form Wizard will create a data form automatically. It is worth building one from scratch, though, to learn how it all fits together.

5 Click on the small button to the right of Select or enter a database name, and browse to the sports.mdb file that you created with Microsoft Access. Leave the other options at the default values. Click Test Connection and you should see a message, Test Connection Succeeded. Click OK to close the dialog.

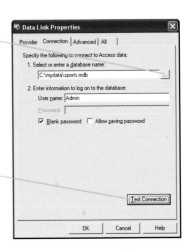

6 Back in the Data Form Wizard, click Next to show the Choose tables or views form. On the left-hand side, click on Members to select it. Then click the right arrow, so it moves to the right-hand list. Click Next to continue.

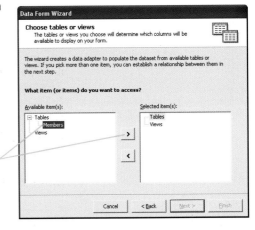

Don't click Finish on this form, as there are some important options in the next part of the Wizard.

7 In the next step, you choose the fields or columns to be displayed on the data form. Leave all the fields checked and click Next.

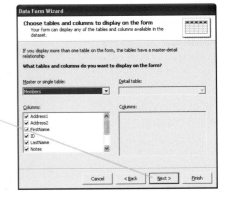

The Grid option uses the DataGrid to show records in a scrolling grid.

The wizard shouldn't really warn about this password since it is blank anyway. In a more advanced application, the database would be secured with a password and the application would prompt the user to enter it at runtime.

8 In the display style form, select the option Single record. Leave all the other options checked. Then click Finish to complete the Data Form Wizard. If you are warned about including a password, click Include... (since this is only a tutorial).

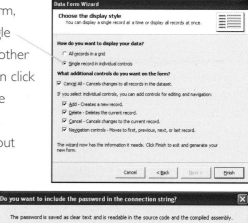

9 If you run the project now, the DataForm will not appear. The reason is that it is not the startup form. Open the code for the main project form, by default Form1.cs. Find the Main method and change Form1 to DataForm1 (or the name of the DataForm). You may want to move the Main method to DataForm1.cs, but this is optional.

The Data Form Wizard is the quickest way to get started with a database application, but once you become familiar with Visual C# you will more often build your own data forms for greater flexibility.

10 When the form runs, click Load to show the data. There are forward and back buttons to navigate. Click Add to add a blank record, fill in the new values, then click Update to save them.

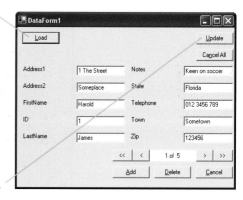

Improving the DataForm

The DataForm generated by the Wizard has three striking weaknesses:

- The fields are in alphabetical order, rather than a logical order

- The records are not sorted

- There is no way to search the database

Here is a quick way to improve the form the Wizard generated. The code is short but not always simple, so there is no need to understand it fully at this stage.

Another idea is to change the Font property of the form, or to make the font of more important fields such as FirstName and LastName bold so they stand out more.

The Search button has its Enabled property set to False, because the search will not work until the data is loaded and sorted. It is enabled in the code for the Load button.

1 Add a Search button and set its Name to btnSearch and Enabled to False. Add a TextBox and call it txtSearch, again set Enabled to false.

2 Use the mouse to reorder the labels and textboxes.

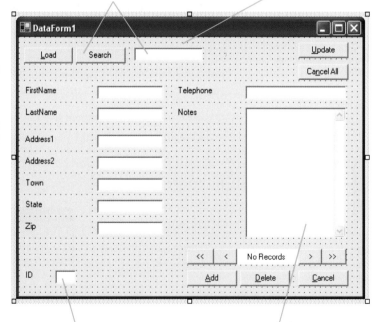

3 Tuck the ID field away as it is normally not necessary to see it.

4 Set the Notes TextBox Multiline property to True and Scrollbars to Vertical as it may have a lot of text.

5 Now double-click the Load button to open its Click event handler. Scroll to the top of the class, and add the line:

```
using System.Data;
```

to the **using** list if it is not already present. Then return to the Click event handler for Load. After the existing line, "this.LoadDataSet();", add the following code:

```
CurrencyManager cm = (CurrencyManager)
        BindingContext[objdsSportsClub, "Members"];
DataView dv= (DataView)cm.List;
dv.Sort = "LastName";
btnSearch.Enabled = true;
txtSearch.Enabled = true;
```

It is important to insert the code at exactly the right point. Otherwise it will not work.

6 Next, double-click the Search button (which you added) to open its Click event handler. Add this code:

```
string SearchName;
int iPosition ;
SearchName = txtSearch.Text.Trim();
if (SearchName != "") {
    CurrencyManager cm =(CurrencyManager)
    BindingContext[objdsSportsClub, "Members"];
    DataView dv = (DataView)cm.List;
    iPosition = dv.Find(SearchName);
    if ( iPosition > -1) {
            BindingContext[objdsSportsClub,
            "Members"].Position = iPosition;
            objdsSportsClub_PositionChanged();
    }
    else MessageBox.Show("No exact match");
    }
}
```

How does this code work? First, it gets the DataView object which Visual c# is using to display the records. Next, it uses the Find method to search it. This only works because the DataView is already sorted on the LastName field, through the code in Step 2. If found, the code moves to that position in the datatable. Don't worry if the code seems somewhat obscure – it is!

7 Test the code by running the application, click Load, and then do a search.

What is disconnected data?

Visual C#'s database library is called ADO.NET. It uses a disconnected data model. This means that the database connection is only used when retrieving or updating data. Operations like navigating through the data, or even adding and changing records, can all be done without going back to the source database. Of course, these changes will be lost if your program doesn't specifically update the database at some point.

You can see this working with the application generated by the DataForm Wizard. In this application, the only buttons that cause a database connection to be made are Load and Update. You can use edit records, and use Add and Delete, as much as you like, but nothing changes in the Access database until you click Update. Another option is to choose Cancel All, which reverts the database back to what it was when last Updated.

Only the Load and Update buttons cause a database connection

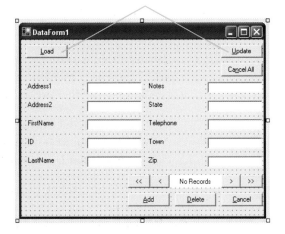

The disconnected database model makes desktop database programming more complex. The advantage is that it is better suited to database programs that work on laptops or across the Internet.

The disconnected database model means that ADO.NET has its own database manager. Rather than simply connecting to a database, ADO.NET imports the data into its own database manager, represented by the DataSet object. The DataSet keeps a record of any changes and additions you make. When you want to update the source database, the code exports these changes back. Although it may seem laborious at first, this approach does have some big advantages.

Why disconnected data?

The disconnected method of database programming has these important advantages:

The aim of this chapter is only to introduce database programming. For advanced work you will need other books, or a careful study of Visual Studio's documentation.

- Since ADO.NET has its own database manager, you can program database applications in the same way no matter what source database you are using. The only parts that vary are the connections and the code that imports data and exports changed data

- The disconnected model is ideal for laptop users, or for connecting to databases over a slow dial-up link. Once the data is loaded, the performance is great because it does not use the network

- The disconnected model makes it easy to undo or cancel database edits, because no permanent updates take place until you choose to make them

There are also some disadvantages:

- With a shared database, you will not see changes made by other users until the data is reloaded

- Because there is a time-lag between editing the data, and updating it back to the database, you are more likely to hit problems such as trying to update a record that was deleted by another user

- A badly programmed application may try to retrieve too much data, causing poor performance or even failure

ADO.NET will not save data to disk automatically. You have to write code that calls the WriteXML method of the Dataset.

The important thing is that as the programmer, you are in control. If it is important to do so, you can write code that connects to the source database every time a record is displayed, and which updates the database after every edit. Equally you can have applications that might run for a week without connecting back to the database. ADO.NET can save the current state of the data to disk, so users can shut down without losing changes. ADO.NET is complex, but gives programmers the flexibility to create database programs to suit every need.

Explaining database objects

If you look at the application generated by the DataForm Wizard, you will notice that it adds three non-visual objects. These are a Connection, a DataAdapter, and a Dataset. The exact type of the objects depends on the type of connection. The example used an OLEDB connection, so the objects include OleDbConnection and OleDbDataAdapter. The Dataset is the same whatever connection is used.

iDBConnection, iDBCommand and iDbDataAdapter are interfaces. The names of the actual classes which implement the interfaces vary from one data provider to another, although they are usually similar, for example OleDbConnection, OleDbCommand etc.

iDbConnection

A connection object manages the link to the source database. A frequently used property is the ConnectionString, which has the information needed to find the database. Important methods are Open and Close.

iDbCommand

Although not used in the example, this is an important object which represents an SQL query or command. It has three Execute... methods which run the statement or query.

iDbDataAdapter

The DataAdapter does the work of importing and exporting data between the Dataset (see below) and the source database. It has four Command (iDBCommand) properties, which represent the SQL commands needed to select, update, delete and insert data.

Dataset

The Dataset is best thought of as ADO.NET's native local database manager. Like other database managers, it can manage one or more database tables, which are represented by DataTable objects. When you read data from a Dataset, you do so by reading data from one of its DataTables.

DataTable

The DataTable represents a set of records. It does not necessarily match a table in a source database. Often, a DataTable is the result of a query spanning several tables in the source.

DataView

The DataView is a view of a DataTable. It allows you to sort and filter the records. You can bind Windows Forms controls to a DataView, for a sorted or filtered view of the data.

Showing data in a grid

The DataGrid is one of the most useful controls in Visual C#. It shows data in a grid view, similar to a spreadsheet. Here is how you can get the Sports Club membership listed in a grid:

1 If you followed the example on page 151, then the sports.mdb connection will be listed in the Server Explorer, under Data Connections. If not, right-click the Data Connections heading, choose Add Connection and set it up using the Data Link Properties dialog (steps 4–5 on pages 151-152.)

2 Add a DataGrid and three buttons to the form. Set the Name property of the buttons to btnLoad, btnUpdate and btnCancel. Set the Text property to Load, Update and Cancel.

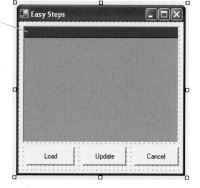

3 From the Data section of the Toolbox choose the OleDbDataAdapter and drag it to the form. The OleDbDataAdapter does the job of retrieving data from the database and passing it to your program. It also handles data in the other direction, sending updates back to the database. When you drag a DataAdapter to a project, it fires off the Configuration Wizard – see over.

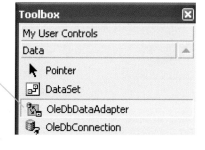

4 From the first screen of the Wizard, click Next.

5 In the next screen, choose the ACCESS sports.mdb database connection from the drop-down list. If you lack the right connection, the New Connection button lets you create it.

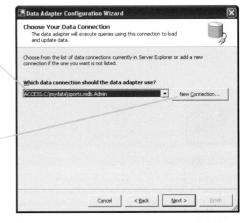

6 This screen determines how the DataAdapter communicates requests and updates data from the database. The two options are SQL statements and stored procedures. Access does not have stored procedures, so just click Next to continue.

7 This is where you determine what data to retrieve. You can either type in an SQL SELECT statement, or do it the visual way by clicking Query Builder. You can use the Query Builder without knowing SQL. Click Query Builder.

SQL stands for Structured Query Language. It is commonly used not just in ADO.NET but throughout the software world.

8 When you choose Query Builder, the Add Table dialog appears. Select the Members table and click Add. Then click Close.

9 In the Query Builder, check the fields that you want to appear in the grid. They appear in the order that you check; or you can change the order later by dragging the row button.

It's usually best not to include a Memo field like Notes in a grid. Grids are poor for longer sections of text.

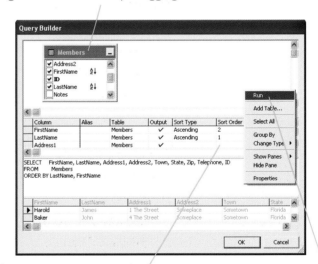

The Query Builder can help you to learn SQL. All the changes you make appear in the SQL language in the center pane. You can also change the SQL directly, and the results show up in the visual part.

10 Click here to set the order of the data. You can choose more than one field. Here the records are ordered by LastName and then FirstName.

11 Right-click and choose Run to test the query. The results appear at the foot of the window. Click OK to continue.

These steps so far apply for all kinds of database applications, not just those where a grid is being used. What you have set up is a data source that can be linked to any of the Visual C# controls.

12 When you close the Query Builder, the SQL is copied into the Configuration Wizard. Click Next to continue. The Configuration Wizard shows a summary dialog. Click Finish to close. If you then see a password dialog, click Include Password.

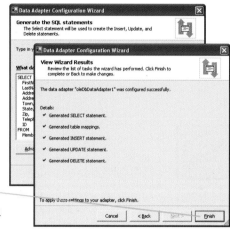

13 Right-click the DataAdapter and choose Generate Dataset. When prompted, choose a New Dataset and call it dsMembers. Leave the option "Add this dataset to the designer" checked, and click OK.

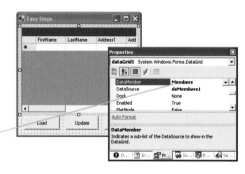

14 Select the Datagrid and set its Datasource property to DsMembers1. Set its DataMember property to Members. In both cases you can pick from a list.

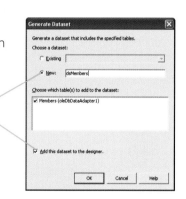

If you try running the Datagrid example, you'll see that no data is displayed. Although the Datagrid is linked to the dataset, the dataset itself has not been filled with data. The DataAdapter only brings back the data when the program specifically requests it. Therefore, a small amount of code is needed.

15 Double-click the Load, Update and Cancel buttons in turn, to generate Click event handlers. Then add the code shown:

To make this into a professional program, you need to deal with any errors that might arise. See page 118.

```
DataGridExample.Form1                    btnLoad_Click(object sender,System.EventArgs e)

    private void btnLoad_Click(object sender, System.EventArgs e)
    {
        dsMembers1.Clear();
        oleDbDataAdapter1.Fill(dsMembers1);
    }

    private void btnUpdate_Click(object sender, System.EventArgs e)
    {
        oleDbDataAdapter1.Update(dsMembers1);
    }

    private void btnCancel_Click(object sender, System.EventArgs e)
    {
        dsMembers1.RejectChanges();
    }
```

16 Run the application and click Load to see the data. Click on the bottom row in the grid (marked with a star) to add a new record. Click anywhere in the grid to edit a record. Click Update to save changes back to the database. Click Cancel to cancel any changes since the last Load.

Cancel will undo all the changes since the last Load, not just the row you are working on. If you add ten records, and then click Cancel, they will all disappear.

Styling a Datagrid

The default grid appearance is plain, but a feature called Tablestyles makes it easy to produce clearer, more attractive formats. Here is how to use Tablestyles to enhance the example Datagrid application:

1 Select a Datagrid, and in the Properties window click the small button to open the editor for the Tablestyles collection.

The key to success when working with TableStyle and ColumnStyle objects is to use the right MappingName. If you are not getting the right results, check the MappingNames.

2 Click the Add button to create a new Tablestyle. Set the HeaderFont to bold. Set the Alternating BackColor to LightBlue (on the Web tab in the Color Selection pop-up). Then scroll down the properties to set the MappingName to Members. Then click the small button to open the GridColumnCollection editor.

If you apply a Tablestyle, the only columns that appear are those for which a GridColumnStyle is included. If you don't add the GridColumnStyles, you can end up with a grid that does not display any columns at all.

3 In the GridColumnCollection editor, click Add for each field you want to appear in the grid. Set the MappingName to the field required. Set the Header Text as required. OK the editors and run to see the new Grid.

Dealing with large databases

The example Datagrid application works well for a small database, but if you have thousands or even hundreds of thousands of rows it will either become very slow or fail completely. The secret of fast database applications is to limit the amount of data travelling between your program and the database.

The SQL Where clause

This query demonstrates two useful SQL tips. One is to use single quotes to include literal characters within the double quotes that mark the C# string. The other is to use the % character as a wildcard, matching any string.

You can reduce the amount of data returned by the DataAdapter by adding a Where clause to its SQL Select statement. For example, you could add the following line to the code for loading the data:

```
oleDbDataAdapter1.SelectCommand.CommandText =
"SELECT FirstName, LastName, Address1, Address2, Town,
State, Zip, Telephone, ID " +
"FROM Members WHERE LastName like 'A%' " +
"ORDER BY LastName, FirstName";
```

To save typing errors, you can use the Query Builder to generate SQL and copy it to your code. SQL statements are not case-sensitive, although the values in the WHERE clause may be case-sensitive with some databases.

If you add this before calling the Fill method, then only those members with names beginning with A will be returned. To make this more useful, you could set up a function with the criteria letter passed in as an argument. You could have the user type in the search letter, or have a row of buttons with a letter of the alphabet on each button, so the user could return all the names matching the button pressed. With a very large database, you could restrict the results still further by using a longer string, or insisting that the user enters a complete LastName before any results are returned.

Limiting Fields

Another way to reduce the amount of data is by selecting fewer fields. For example, you could have a separate button to show the full address of a member, and limit the grid to just FirstName, LastName, Telephone and ID. However much you limit the fields, it is important to include the Primary Key, in this case the ID field. Otherwise you will not be able to look up other data about the selected row, or update the data, because there is no unique identifier.

Copying a record to the Clipboard

A handy technique if you have a database of addresses is to be able to copy an address to the Windows Clipboard. Then you can easily paste it into a document, for example a letter.

The Clipboard object

The .NET Framework has an invisible Clipboard object. It has methods for setting or retrieving its contents. In this example, all you need is the SetDataObject method, which adds data to the clipboard.

The example also shows how to get the data in the selected row programmatically. Once you know the index of the selected row, you can drill down to that row in the DataSet. The DataSet has a Tables collection, which in this case has only one Table, so it must be index 0. Each Table has a Rows collection, and each row has a collection of fields.

Adding a Clipboard button

Add a button named "btnClip" to the data form and give it the Text "Clip".

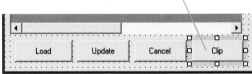

Note the use of the \n character, which represents a carriage return.

Double-click the button to open its Click event, and enter the following code:

```
string Address;
int i   = dataGrid1.CurrentRowIndex;
if (i != -1)
{
DataRow dr = dsMembers1.Tables[0].Rows[i];
Address = dr["FirstName"] + " ";
Address += dr["LastName"] +"\n";
Address += dr["Address1"] +"\n";
//add other fields as needed
Clipboard.SetDataObject(Address);
MessageBox.Show("The address is on the clipboard");
}
```

This example shows how to place text on the clipboard that will disappear when the application exits. If you add a second argument to SetDataObject, and make it True, then the data persists on the clipboard until specifically cleared.

Creating a report

One essential element of most database projects is a report facility. For example, a sports club might want to print out a members list. Visual Studio comes with an integrated report designer. Here is an example of how to create a telephone list:

Visual C# Standard edition does not include Crystal Reports. You need at least Visual Studio Professional.

Start a new Windows project, choose File > Add new item, and select Crystal Report.

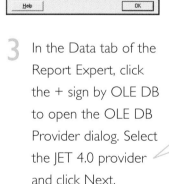

2 When the Crystal Report gallery appears, choose Standard and Using the Report Expert. Then click OK.

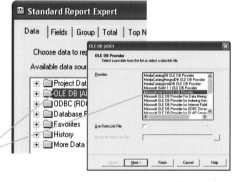

3 In the Data tab of the Report Expert, click the + sign by OLE DB to open the OLE DB Provider dialog. Select the JET 4.0 provider and click Next.

There are plenty of other options for datasources. You can also link a report to a dataset, but to do so involves a little more code than selecting an independent source.

4 Click the small Browse button and select sports.mdb. Then click Finish.

5 Select the Members table from your new OLE DB connection and click Insert Table. Then click Next to continue.

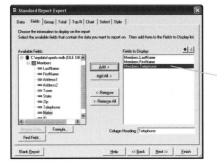

6 Select the fields to display by highlighting the required field in the left-hand list, and clicking Add. For the telephone list, select LastName, FirstName and Telephone. Then click Finish.

Once the database connection has been made, designing a report is like designing a form. Use the Properties editor to edit report objects. Display the Field Explorer to drag-and-drop new report objects, such as additional fields. Right-click the report for a menu of further tools, including sort order. When you are done, save the report.

If the Field Explorer is not visible, show it by selecting View > Other Windows > Document Outline.

Field Explorer   Designer

Pop-up menu, choose Report > Sort Records to sort

Showing a report

1 To show a report in a Visual C# application, first add a new form for the report, using File > Add new item and choosing Windows Form. On the form, place a CrystalReportViewer object. Set its Dock property to Fill.

2 Select the CrystalReportViewer, and in the Properties window select ReportSource. Choose Browse, and select the report you designed.

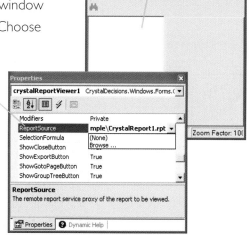

3 On another form in your application, place a Report button. Double-click to open its Click event handler, and add the following code:

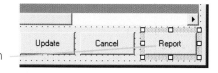

```
Form2 f = new Form2();
f.Show();
```

4 Run the project, and click the button to show the report.

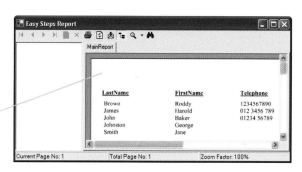

The next step with databases

Visual C# is a little harder to use than standalone database applications like Microsoft Access, but has several advantages. One is that many of Visual C#'s general development features are also useful in database projects. Another advantage is that if you want to distribute a completed database application, it is easier to do so with Visual C#. With a custom application, it is easier to limit the user's actions to ones that you know are safe for the data, and to present the data in the most effective way.

Working with Access

Visual C# and Microsoft Access make excellent partners. You can use Access to create databases, set up validation rules, and do interactive editing, while using Visual C# to develop a packaged application.

The MSDE Database engine comes with all versions of Visual Studio. It is a cut-down edition of SQL Server.

Getting relational

More advanced databases use several linked tables. For example, a company might use separate tables for customers, orders and products. A database for a CD collection might have tables for CDs, Tracks and Artists. These relational databases give more power and flexibility, but are substantially harder to manage than single-table databases like the Sports Club example.

Going Client-Server

Wondering what sort of driver to use? Generally, a native ADO.NET provider is the best choice if one is available.

ADO.NET supports several database technologies, including ADO.NET, OLE DB, and ODBC. ODBC stands for Open DataBase Connectivity. To connect to a particular database, you need a suitable ODBC driver. Most major database managers have suitable drivers, from heavyweights like Oracle to open-source alternatives like MySQL. There are also increasing numbers of native ADO.NET providers. Server database systems like SQL Server, Oracle or DB2 require the most complex type of database programming, but are necessary for good performance on large networks, say of 10 or more users.

Connecting to the Web

Through ASP.NET, it is easy to extend C# applications to deliver data over the Internet. Visual C# can keep pace with all your database needs, from small one-user applications to heavyweight enterprise systems.

Running C# on the Internet

This chapter shows how C# makes it possible to build exciting Web projects. Using C#, you can create dynamic Web pages, including rich database applications. This feature is called Web Forms, also known as ASP.NET.

Covers

Chapter Eight

What kind of Web?

A Web is any system where Web browsers can view HTML pages over a network. HTML stands for HyperText Markup Language, and it lets you easily move from one page to another by clicking hyperlinks. The best known network of this kind is the Internet, home of the World Wide Web. But there are different ways in which Web technology is used:

- You may have a private network which includes a Web server. This is called an Intranet

- You may be creating Web pages for the World Wide Web, which you upload to an ISP (Internet Service Provider) to make them available for public view

- You may be part of an organization with a permanent link to the Internet

A problem with the Internet is that different browser versions and computer platforms make it hard to create Web pages that have the same features everywhere. If you are using an Intranet, it is easier to control what browsers your users have. ASP.NET can work well with any browser, but some features only work with Internet Explorer. This is OK on an Intranet but not on the World Wide Web. If you are using Web Forms, you can set the Target Schema for maximum compatibility.

Web pages need not be static documents and can allow you to query databases, place orders or play games. Most things that can be done with traditional applications can also be done on Web pages. In the .NET Framework, dynamic web pages are called Web Forms. These let you write Visual C# code that runs on a Windows web server. Like Windows Forms, Web Forms can have buttons, text boxes, database grids, and so on. ASP.NET lets you write code for these in much the same way as you would in a Windows Forms application.

ASP.NET also supports a technology called web services. This lets you write applications in C# (or other languages) that communicate with other applications over the Internet, without the involvement of a browser or a an HTML page. C# clients can also use web services created in other languages such as Java.

A key advantage of ASP.NET applications is that when carefully designed they work with any computer that can run a web browser. For example, in a network of mixed Windows, Linux and Macintosh machines, all the users could access the same web application.

Introducing Web Forms

A Web Form is the same as an ASP.NET page. In order to use Web Forms, you must have a Windows Web server on your network, that has the .NET Framework installed. You can install this on your own machine, and it is an option in the Visual Studio setup. Alternatively, if you are on an Intranet, there may be a Web server elsewhere on the network that you can use. For full Visual Studio support, there are other special requirements such as the FrontPage extensions. Permissions also have to be configured correctly to support ASP.NET debugging. If you are installing on your own machine, the Visual Studio setup will configure the server for you.

Having a Web server installed can be a security risk when you dial the Internet.
Check Microsoft's website for the latest security information about Internet Information Server.

A word about deployment

If you want to do more than just experiment with Web forms, you will want to deploy your work. On an Intranet that is no problem. If you want to publish to the Web, then you need an ISP that supports the .NET Framework (unless you are lucky enough to have your own Web server permanently connected and open to the Internet). Some ISPs charge extra for ASP.NET services, while others may not support it at all. In order to support ASP.NET, the ISP must offer Windows web servers, rather than UNIX or Linux. There are also variations in terms of exactly what is available on the ISP's web server. Choose an ISP carefully, to ensure that the services and database that you need are available to you.

In order to keep costs down, most ISPs offer shared hosting. This means that other ASP.NET web sites are running on the same server. Although this works well, it is another reason why there will be restrictions on what you can do. To avoid the compromises involved, you can rent a dedicated server, but this is much more expensive. ASP.NET applications are designed to be published on the Internet. This means that security is paramount, especially if the applications involve commercial transactions or access to private information. Programming secure applications takes extra care. Things to look out for include features that let users write information to the web server's hard disk, or data that is typed in and then used in SQL queries, or the facility to send emails from a web site. Careful handling of passwords is vital. Before deploying to the Internet, study the security information in the Visual Studio.NET documentation and on Microsoft's web site.

Creating a Web Form

These examples assume you have set up a Web server on your machine. The Web address "localhost" means the machine on which Visual Studio is running.

If you get an error at this stage, check the Web address carefully. The example assumes a local Web server, but you may be using one on another machine. If Visual Studio finds the Web server, but cannot create the project files, check the configuration of the Web server, permissions, and that the .NET Framework is installed.

When you set the target schema for the solution, it does not automatically update the web form that has already been created. Check the TargetSchema property for WebForm1.aspx and amend if needed.

JScript is compatible with JavaScript, a scripting language used by all the main web browsers.

From the File menu, choose New Project and select ASP .NET Web Application. In the Location box, type:

```
http://localhost/
EasyWeb
```

Then click OK.

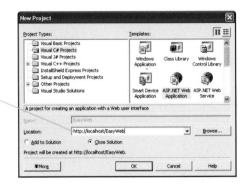

You will see this dialog while Visual Studio creates the necessary files on the Web server.

Open the Solution Explorer, right-click the name of the project and choose

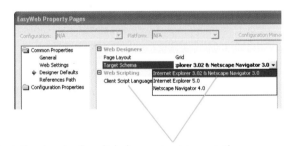

Properties. Right at the beginning, it is important to set the Target Schema. If you are targeting the public Web, normally choose the Internet Explorer 3.02 and Navigator 3.0 option. If you are targeting an Intranet or just learning ASP.NET, it is fine to choose Internet Explorer 5.0. Leave the client script at JScript for the Web, and normally also for Intranets unless you have a good reason to use VB Script. In ASP.NET, most of the client script is generated for you, so it does not matter if you don't know JScript.

4 Select the Web Forms section of the Toolbox and drag a ListBox, a TextBox and a Button to the form.

The HTML view of a Web form lets you edit the HTML source that makes up the Web page. Any changes you make are reflected in the design view as well. It is often best to let Visual Studio generate most of the HTML, but sometimes changes have to be made manually.

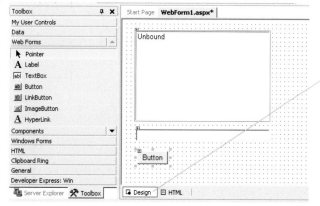

Make sure the Web Form is in Design mode (tab at bottom of Designer)

5 Select the Button and press F4 to display its properties. Set the Text property to Add item.

6 Double-click the button to open its Click event handler. There will be a pause while Visual C# creates a "code-behind" file. Then the code editor opens.

A code-behind file is a C# class that is linked to the Web page. In practise, it works in the same way as the code view of a Windows form.

7 Here is the code for the Click event handler:

```
string s = TextBox1.Text.Trim();
    if (s != string.Empty) {
    ListBox1.Items.Add(s);
    }
TextBox1.Text = string.Empty;
```

8 Return to the Design view, click on a blank part of the Web Form and press F4. The Properties Explorer should say DOCUMENT; if it does not, select DOCUMENT from the drop-down list. Here you can amend the properties of the page. Change the Title to Web Pages in Easy Steps.

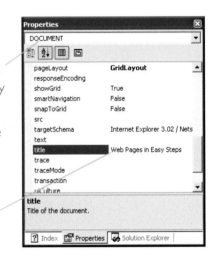

9 Run the project. Enter some text in the text box and click Add item. The text you type appears in the list. Note that the title of the page appears in the browser. An interesting thing to do is to right-click the page in the

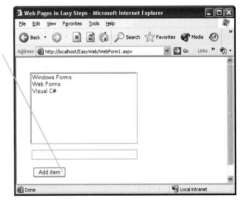

browser and choose Visual Source. There is no script visible. When you click the button, the page is fetched afresh from the Web server. All the code runs on the server.

How Web Forms work

Although it is a simple application, the Web Form you have constructed has some advanced features:

- It runs compiled C# code, not just script code

- When you add an item to the list, the items that were previously added remain as well. Normally, when you refresh a Web page, any information you enter is lost

- Coding the Web Form is very similar to coding a Windows form

How it works

The code behind a Visual C# Web Form application is compiled to a .NET Framework library. When the page is requested by a browser, the Web server reads the Web page (normally with an .aspx extension) and interprets any special tags. In addition, it fires events that are handled by the code-behind class, and which can modify the contents of the page that gets returned to the browser.

Managing state

If you look at the source of an ASP .NET page in the browser (not the source in Visual C#), you can see the VIEWSTATE field. It is plain text and does not require any special browser features. It can be quite large, and some Web forms are optimized by reducing the use of VIEWSTATE.

In addition, the page has a hidden field called VIEWSTATE. The current value of the controls on the page is encoded into this field. When the user clicks a button on the form, the Web server is able to read back the previous state of the controls on the page through VIEWSTATE. ASP.NET generates a new version of the page incorporating both the VIEWSTATE values and any new changes. This way, there could be dozens of users using the site at the same time, each one adding different values to the list, and each user will get their own list back from the Web server.

For success with Web Forms, it is important to remember that although you can code them in a similar way to Windows forms, state is managed in this different way. In addition, there is a feature called Session state, that lets you store variables linked to the current user. Other than through special techniques like these, objects do not retain their values between page requests. After all, the next page request might be for a different user.

The Web Forms Toolbox

When working with Web Forms, there are three sections on the Toolbox that you will use most frequently:

The **Web Forms section** is for rich ASP.NET controls. These range from simple objects like labels and TextBoxes, through to advanced controls like the calendars and the DataGrid. These controls must run on the Web server. You can write code against them in the same way as for Windows Form controls

Why not run all HTML controls at the server? The reason is that this is a little slower. If you don't need program control, a plain HTML control is the fastest option.

The **HTML section** is for standard HTML controls, but with an important difference. You can design a Web page visually with these controls, in the same way as with other Web design tools like FrontPage. The difference is that by right-clicking one of these controls and choosing Run as server control, you can handle events and code their properties just as for Web Form controls

One of the best features of ASP .NET is easy access to data. The **Data Section** is applicable to Web Forms just as it is to Windows Forms

The Page Class and Code-behind

The ASP.NET Page class represents a dynamic web page. For each ASP.NET web form you create, Visual Studio usually generates two files. The first has the extension .aspx and does not contain any C# code. It looks like an HTML file, and when you design a page in the web form designer, corresponding HTML code appears in the .aspx document.

It is not essential to use code-behind. You can also put C# code in the .aspx file, surrounded with special tags. But code-behind is normally preferred, as it separates the program code from the tags that define the page layout.

The second file has the same name but with .cs appended, and is pure C#. This second file is a class which inherits from Page, and by modifying its behavior you can control the content that the end user sees in their web browser. This is called the code-behind file. When you add a control in the web form designer, a matching C# object appears in the code-behind file. To see this at work, try the following example.

1. In Visual Studio, start a new web application. Right-click the web form in the designer and choose View Code.

2. Look at the code-behind and note that it has no protected members. Now go back to the web form designer, add a Label control, and View Code again. Visual Studio generates a class member of type Label. Add some code to the Page_Load event handler to set the Label's Text property.

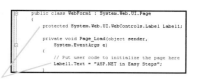

If the text is static like this, you could simply set the Text property in the web form designer, or use an HTML Label. The power of the C# code is that the text can be programmatically controlled, for example to display values from a database.

3. Run the project to see how the code you wrote ends up as a line of text in the web browser.

The Load event and isPostBack

When a user requests a page, the Page Load event fires. The code here runs before the page is sent to the browser, so you can use it to initialize variables and properties as required.

An ASP.NET is designed to work in a similar way to a Windows form, although in reality the Web is a very different platform. For example, you might write some code for a button click event that changes the text of a label. What really happens is that the page is submitted to the web server as a form. ASP.NET then regenerates the page, including the change made in the click event handler. This mechanism means the Page_Load event fires every time an event such as a button click occurs, and not just when the user first navigates to the page. This can have two undesirable side-effects. First, the initialization code for a page can be quite substantial, including multiple database queries. Running this every time the page is refreshed by a button click means slow performance. Second, the Page_Load event can overwrite values that you want to preserve.

Event handling code for controls always runs after Page_Load, so you can be sure that changes made specifically in control event handlers can not be overwritten.

For example, say you have a button and a textbox on a form, and the value of the textbox is set to a default value in Page_Load. Now the user types in some different text for the textbox, and clicks the button. The Page_Load event will set the textbox back to its default value.

Understanding isPostBack

Make sure you understand isPostBack and check its value where needed. Otherwise, your ASP.NET application will probably not work correctly.

In order to overcome this problem, the Page class has an isPostBack property. If isPostBack is true, it means the page request has been generated by an event on the page itself, such as a button click. Normally, that means there is no need to re-initialize page controls. Typical code for Page_Load looks like this:

```csharp
if (!this.IsPostBack)
    {
    this.TextBox1.Text = "Some default value";
    //other initialization code
    }
```

This ensures that the initialization code only runs when the page is first loaded, and not in response to every event.

The Session object

The Page class has many useful properties, methods and events. One is the Session object. This lets you store objects and variables that are associated with the current user.

The problem of tracking the user

A web server delivers pages one by one. If it receives two requests for pages within a short space of time, it does not know whether they are from the same user, or different users. In order for web applications to work, it is essential to overcome this problem and to keep track of the user. Behind the scenes, there are a number of ways to do this including cookies, which allow the web server to store variables on the user's computer, and encoded URLs, which identify the user by long codes added to the web address.

Although you can store any object as a session variable, its unwise to store very large objects such as big datasets. They will stay in memory for at least 20 minutes, and on a busy site that would consume too many resources.

ASP.NET wraps this technology behind a property of the Page class called Session. You can store one or more variables of any type in the Session object. The values persist until the Session expires, which by default is 20 minutes after the time of the last request in the session. You can also end a session by calling the Abandon method.

A Session Example

Start a new web application and add four Labels, three TextBoxes and a button to the default web form as shown. Set the ID property of the TextBoxes to txtName,

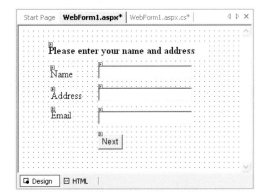

txtAddress and txtEmail. Set the ID of the Button to btnNext. Change the Text properties as shown.

For more information on creating classes, see page 77 and following.

2 Go to File > Add New Item, and add a second web form to the project. Next, select File > Add New Item again and add a class called EasyStepsUser.cs. Give the EasyStepsUser class Name, Address and Email properties of type string.

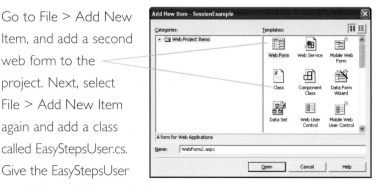

Note the use of Response.Redirect to redirect the browser to a different page.

3 In the design view, double-click btnNext and add the code shown to its Click event handler. The code creates a new EasyStepsUser object, based on the values in the textboxes, and saves it as an item in the Session object. Session is a property of the Page class. Note that you could improve this code by adding validation, to check for appropriate values in the textboxes.

```
private void btnNext_Click(object sender,
    System.EventArgs e) {
    EasyStepsUser user = new EasyStepsUser();
    user.Name = this.txtName.Text;
    user.Address = this.txtAddress.Text;
    user.Email = this.txtEmail.Text;

    if (this.Session["currentUser"] != null) {
        this.Session.Remove("currentUser");
    }

    this.Session.Add("currentUser",user);

    //open the next page
    this.Response.Redirect("WebForm2.aspx");
}
```

4 Now open the design view of WebForm2.aspx and add two labels as shown. Set the ID property of the second label to lbMessage.

5 Double-click WebForm2.aspx to open its Page_Load event handler. Add the code shown.

```
private void Page_Load(object sender, System.EventArgs e) {
    EasyStepsUser user;
    if (this.Session["currentUser"] != null) {
        user = (EasyStepsUser)Session["currentUser"];
        this.lbMessage.Text  = "Welcome, " + user.Name
            + ", your email is: " + user.Email;
    }
    else {
        this.Response.Redirect("WebForm1.aspx");
    }
}
```

Once a web application has been run within Visual Studio, you can also run it directly from the browser. Simply open up a web browser and navigate to the application's URL.

6 Test the application by running it, entering some values on WebForm1, and clicking Next to view WebForm2. If the user goes directly to WebForm2, bypassing WebForm1, the application redirects to the first page because there is no currentUser object in the Session.

More about the Session object

The Session object is particularly useful because it can store any kind of object. However, because it is a collection of the base object type, you must use casting to access the properties and methods of the object you stored.

The object remains in the Session until either you remove it or the session expires. In this example, imagine the user gets to the second page, and then realizes that there is an error in the details. If they click Back and then refresh the page, all the field values disappear. You could overcome this by adding code to the Page_Load event of WebForm1.aspx that checks for the existence of a currentUser object, and if found sets the values of the textboxes accordingly. Then the user can click forward and back and everything behaves as expected, even if the page is refreshed.

If the user closes the browser, the session ends. The web server does not know that the browser has closed, but the old Session object will become inaccessible.

ASP.NET and databases

ADO.NET, the .NET database library, is the same for ASP.NET as it is for Windows Forms. It is possible to write data access classes that can be used as part of both Windows and Web applications. However, although the non-visual database classes such as DataSets and DataTables are the same, the controls that display data are different on web forms. It is also important to understand how ASP.NET sessions work (see pages 181-183) so that you can keep track of things like current database rows in web applications.

Deploying a database

If you have a choice between JET or SQL Server, use SQL Server. It has better security and better performance. The MDB has one advantage, which is that you can easily upload and download the data.

There are two database engines supplied with Visual C#, along with drivers for other database servers. The two supplied engines are Microsoft Access, also known as JET, and a version of SQL Server called the Microsoft Database Engine or MSDE. Some versions of Visual Studio come with a full developer version of SQL Server. JET and SQL Server are both widely used with ASP.NET.

In order to get database applications working in ASP.NET, it is important to get the security aspect right. Follow these guidelines:

1. If you are using an online database through your ISP, follow the ISP's directions. You may be given a database username and password for SQL Server, or there may be instructions on how to upload and query Access MDB databases.

If you are on a network, note that the ASPNET account is not a network account, but only exists on the local machine. That means by default it cannot access network shares or SQL Server databases elsewhere on the network. To do this you need to change the account being used for data access, using one of the advanced authentication techniques in ASP.NET.

2. If you are running ASP.NET on your own network, and wish to query an Access MDB, you must ensure that the ASP.NET user account, which is usually called ASPNET, has read and write access to the folder where the MDB is located. This will not be the case by default. Right-click the folder containing the MDB, choose Sharing and Security, then the Security tab. Find the ASP account and give it read and write access. Execute rights are not required.

3. If you are using SQL Server or MSDE, you can either use password-based security or Windows-based security. If using password-based security, simply use the correct user name and password. If it is Windows-based security, you will either need to give the ASPNET user access to the database, or else use one of the more advanced authentication techniques in ASP.NET.

Showing data in a DataGrid

1. Start a new ASP .NET project and call it EasyData. Set the TargetSchema as shown on page 174. Then place a DataGrid on the form.

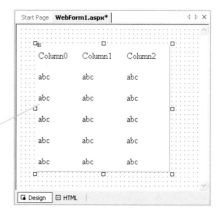

2. If you followed the Sports Club example on page 151, you will have the connection to sports.mdb in the Server Explorer. If not, follow the procedures there to

create it, or a connection to another database. Drag the Members table to the form. It will create two new objects, OleDbConnection1 and OleDbDataAdapter1.

If you prefer you can use the Query Builder as described on page 161.

3. Right-click the DataAdapter and open the Configuration Wizard by selecting Configure Data Adapter. Select the existing data connection. In the SQL Select field, type:

```
SELECT FirstName,
LastName, Town,
Telephone, ID FROM
Members ORDER BY
LastName, FirstName
```

Accept the other defaults and close the Wizard.

4 Right-click the DataAdapter and choose Generate Dataset. Call the Dataset dsMembers. Then close with OK.

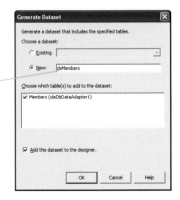

This application makes no use of the Data key field. It is useful when you want to get the primary key of a record from a row in the DataGrid, without having to display the key.

5 It is now possible to configure the DataGrid. Right-click the control and choose Property Builder. On the General tab, set DataSource to DsMembers1, DataMember to Members, and DataKeyField to ID.

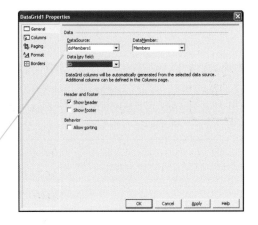

If you have columns generated automatically, it is inflexible. In addition, you can easily end up with some columns repeated.

6 Next, click the Columns section. Uncheck the option to Create columns automatically at run time. Then select all the columns except ID. For FirstName and LastName, change the Header text to add a space between the words.

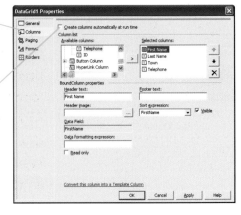

7 Next, select the Format section. Click Header and check Bold.

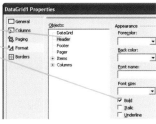

8 Expand the Items section and select Alternating Items. Click Back color and select a light color for the background of alternate rows.

9 Close the Property Builder and double-click the Web Form to open the code-behind

```csharp
private void Page_Load(object sender, System.EventArgs e)
{
    // Put user code to initialize the page here

    if (! IsPostBack)
    {
        this.oleDbDataAdapter1.Fill(dsMembers1);
        this.DataBind();
    }
}
```

at the Page Load event handler. Add the code shown.

10 Run the application. Here, a label has been added to the form to make a heading. This is live data from the Access database; if the data is modified, the page will change next time it is refreshed.

Where next?

You have come to the end of *C# in easy steps*, but there is plenty more to learn and achieve. Here are some tips:

1. Start a project

It is hard to learn how to program if you have no clear goal. Find a project, whether at home, in the office, or at a club, and work out how to use C# to create a solution. Even if your first attempt is not completely successful, you will learn a lot by solving the real-world problems it throws up.

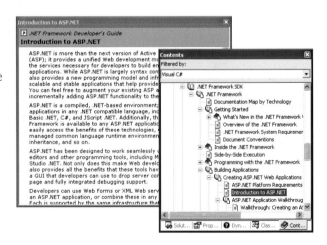

When you look for help on the Internet, include C# or dotnet in the search. There are a lot of differences between .NET programming and more general Windows development.

2. Get help

Whatever problem you have, the chances are that someone, somewhere has tackled it before. Because C# is so popular, you can easily find help in books and on the Internet. Microsoft runs Internet newsgroups on Visual C# and the .NET Framework technologies where you can ask questions.

3. Test and improve

In business, the customer is always right. In software, the user is always right. If your C# program is to be used by others, get them to try it out and report back the problems they have. Even better, watch them working and see how you can make the software more productive, by cutting down the number of steps needed to perform some task, or improving the screen layout, or speeding performance at critical points.

Don't ignore the most obvious source of help: Visual Studio's online reference

Index

M

MDI 132
Menu 96
  Pop-up 98
Methods 28, 52, 60
MonthCalendar control 47

N

Name hiding 88
Namespace 54, 91
New 61

O

Objects 14, 76–77
Object type 55–56
OpenFileDialog 40–41
Operators 52
Outlining 102
Overloading 88
Overriding 88

P

Page class 179
Parameters 52, 60, 73
PictureBox 32
Printing 126
Professional Edition (Visual Studio .NET) 8
Projects
  Creating new 12
  Opening 26
  Saving 25

Project properties 114
Properties 19, 52
Properties window 12, 14
Property Wizard 79
Protected 90

R

RadioButton 34
Reference manager 112
Reference types 72
Reports 167
RichTextBox 45–46

S

Sbyte 56
Scope 62
Semi-colons 59
Session 181
Setup project 140
Short 56
Solution Explorer 24
Splitter control 44
SQL Server 184
Standard Edition (Visual C#) 8
State
  Managing 177
Statement 52
Static 89
Step Out 107
Step Over 107
String 56
Structs 70
Switch statement 67–68

T

Tab control 43
Tab order 48
Target Schema 174
TextBox 20, 31